The Consumer Mind

The Consumer Mind

Brand perception
and the implication
for marketers

Pepe Martinez

KoganPage

LONDON PHILADELPHIA NEW DELHI

First published in Great Britain and the United States in 2012 by Kogan Page Limited

120 Pentonville Road	1518 Walnut Street, Suite 1100	4737/23 Ansari Road
London N1 9JN	Philadelphia PA 19102	Daryaganj
United Kingdom	USA	New Delhi 110002
www.koganpage.com		India

© Pepe Martinez, 2012

The right of Pepe Martinez to be identified as the author of this work has been asserted by him in accordance with the Copyright, Designs and Patents Act 1988.

ISBN   978 0 7494 6570 4
E-ISBN   978 0 7494 6571 1

British Library Cataloguing-in-Publication Data

A CIP record for this book is available from the British Library.

Library of Congress Cataloging-in-Publication Data

Martinez, Pepe, 1960–
    The consumer mind : brand perception and the implication for marketers / Pepe Martinez.
        p. cm.
    Includes bibliographical references.
    ISBN 978-0-7494-6570-4 – ISBN 978-0-7494-6571-1 (ebook)   1. Consumers–Psychology.
2. Neuromarketing.   3. Branding (Marketing)   4. Marketing–Psychological aspects.   I. Title.
    HF5415.32.M378 2012
    658.8'343–dc23

                                                                                    2012003193

Typeset by Graphicraft Limited, Hong Kong
Print production managed by Jellyfish
Printed and bound by CPI Group (UK) Ltd, Croydon, CR0 4YY

*For all those people who have left
a significant and positive imprint on my mind*

CONTENTS

PREFACE

Perhaps because it distinguishes us from 'the beasts' we humans are inordinately fond of our individual and collective capacity for 'rational' thought. We like to believe we act on the basis of rational thought even though the evidence suggests that we are invariably guided by our 'irrational' instincts and impulses. How else do you explain the success of Tamagotchis, the Macarena or even the iPad?

In this book Pepe Martínez uses everyday examples to explore how instincts, impulses and cognition combine to determine our reaction to the world around us. He brings together the world experienced through the senses and the world as understood by the mind, and explores how the two create meaning, the mental significance that empowers brands and makes them valuable.

This is not an ordinary book on neuroscience. It is a unique exploration of the meaning created by everyday events and encounters set against a backdrop of how our mind works. One that reminds us we are all 'researchers' seeking to understand and make sense of ourselves and our world.

Nigel Hollis
Executive Vice President and Chief Global Analyst, Millward Brown
Fairfield, Connecticut, United States

As marketers we are trying to influence the way our brands are perceived to encourage the trial and repeat purchase. In the pursuit of this aim we use the language of 'consumers', 'shoppers' and 'respondents'. But the reality is that we are dealing with 'people', 'human beings' and those definitions include us and our families and friends.

This book is a field guide for marketers, encouraging us to think about people and their everyday lives and how our increasing understanding of our brains explains how we all behave day to day. It is from this new common sense understanding of how we respond to experiences, what we remember and what we recall, how we decide and how we behave that marketers can refine what they do to make brands more personally relevant to more people.

In *The Consumer Mind* we are not trying to add to the academic literature nor trying to further understanding of the biology of the brain. It is an accessible handbook for marketers and advertisers to connect our daily thoughts and actions with the practice of marketing.

Gordon Pincott
Chairman, Global Solutions, Millward Brown
Warwick, United Kingdom

During my 10 years of training and my 20 years and more of experience in market research, I have been able to see for myself the usefulness of qualitative and quantitative methods in gathering and analysing information offered by consumers.

In later years, an ethnographic (from anthropology) focus allowed us to live with consumers, giving us the opportunity to observe their behaviour 'live and direct', adding another study tool to our arsenal. Now, neuroscience has reached market research and is challenging traditional methods. I was born and live in Poland, a country where this new discipline has been widely welcomed. I have become a huge fan of this focus.

Pepe Martínez is one of the best researchers of our time and truly understands that there are many pathways to reach the 'truth'; the very essence of things. And, most important, that these pathways are complementary.

The Consumer Mind offers us a wealth of exciting and practical knowledge on the phenomena relating to the consumption of brands, products and services. It is also written in a very entertaining and unusual style. Believe me, not reading it would almost be an act of bad taste.

Krzysztof B Kruszewski
Chairman, Firefly Millward Brown Europe
Warsaw, Poland

Pepe's first book *Qualitology* was devoted to the various qualitative research techniques that help marketers to understand better what consumers think and why they think as they do. The book showed the author's passion for understanding human behaviour.

Qualitative techniques look into human nature with the help of tools rooted in clinical psychology; it is obvious that Freudian thinking is not alien to Pepe's mind. Freud is very often regarded by science as not 'scientific' enough to be taken as a base for strong theory. Neuroscience on the other hand is founded on well-grounded neurobiological research. These two paradigms seem to be distant from each other. In his book Pepe has the courage to combine both points of view, enriching them with other psychological concepts on our personality and emotions.

The Consumer Mind is an introduction to neuroscience. From this book one can learn how our brain is built, where the basic structures responsible for reasoning, decision making, emotions and senses are located. This is not for the sake of knowledge itself, however. Pepe describes them to better introduce concepts well known in everyday marketing practice: one has to understand the very origin and nature of memory, attention and emotion to build a brand successfully.

This book is not only about theory, it is more about how this theory is applied in marketing practice, so we learn about how to build brands, how to carry out better research into advertising based on Pepe's examples. This aspect makes *The Consumer Mind* essential reading for everybody who is interested in how the latest developments in science have influenced today's marketing practice.

Pawel Ciacek
Head of Neuroscience Practice, Millward Brown Europe
Warsaw, Poland

Physics versus metaphysics. Body and soul. Brain and mind. For a long time these different concepts have been thought of and felt as separate entities. However, the 21st century is more and more illuminating about their continuum and interdependence.

Matter and energy had been evolving for millions of years until the human mind appeared. And the result is a wonderful and highly sophisticated 'thing' that hosts very different dimensions: biological (the brain as part of our physiological body), psychological (yes, there is someone in our heads!), sociological (our relationships with others) and a historical perspective (the time management of the past, present and future).

In this book, Pepe shows us in a clear and actionable way how our minds work ... from our everyday life to the many lives of brands and communications. Pepe, with whom I have shared great professional experiences and who is also a very good friend, has a passionate curiosity about the mind and the progress of neuroscience. The way he talks about them is always very accessible and fun, but this masks extensive reading and a deep knowledge of the workings of the human mind. So don't be fooled by Pepe's simplicity: he will always know you more than you think you do!

Enjoy reading and take the opportunity to meet the man behind the book in person!

Cécile Conaré
Director, Europe, Firefly Millward Brown
London, United Kingdom

When Pepe told me a few months ago that he was going to write a book about consumers' minds and explained what it was going to contain, two conclusions leapt immediately into my head: finally I am going to find out how our 'control tower' works. I have always been really lazy about learning the terminology that is used to describe it. However, Pepe writes as he speaks, and he speaks very clearly. And finally I would manage to explain to my wife the reasons behind my obsession with buying technology (I love Apple products). I have run out of excuses to justify myself and I need some fresh arguments to be able to continue my 'habit'.

A few weeks ago I was one of the lucky ones to receive a draft copy of this book. So I took the opportunity during a high speed rail journey between Madrid and Barcelona to read it closely. On the outward trip

I read half the book because I found it interesting, enjoyable and easy to read. Later the same day, during my meetings, I found myself reconciling my reasoning with my emotions to offer a balanced argument. Readers will understand this statement when they have finished reading this book.

I really wanted that day in Barcelona to end so that I could use the return journey to read the rest of the book. And that's how it was: when I got home I began to relate to my family with the new insight, outlook and understanding that reading this book had given me.

Now, having read it, I realize that I understand myself a little better, that I understand a bit more about the people who are around me, and I even understand my job a little bit better. I even understand why I recently had to buy my 12-year old son, Javito, a BlackBerry.

Congratulations Pepe! I think you have hit the mark again.

Vicente Condés
Marketing Manager,
APD (Asociación para el Progreso de la Dirección)
Madrid, Spain

This book is a great contribution to professionals working in marketing. It helps us to understand how our work is progressing and the direction it is taking in the 21st century and makes us aware of the need to understand the mental processes of consumers.

Pepe Martínez, as is his custom, guides us through the various different mental processes in a simple and enjoyable way, and he ends each chapter with a brief reflection on the practical application of what we have learnt with regard to brands.

I have always thought being a marketing specialist to be an exciting career: you need a high humanist regard and to understand that, deep down, brands are like people, and this book clearly shows that.

Brands have to be coherent and genuine to be credible. There has to be an understanding between what they think (their values), the emotions they create (what they feel), what they say (their communications) and the actions they carry out (what they do).

Thank you Pepe for reminding us that success is having what you want and happiness is wanting what you have.

Enrique Larumbe
General Manager, Eurogap
San Sebastián, Spain

I'm sure that for many of us – and this is definitely the case for me – the brain seems such a complex organ, capable of so very many things, that it feels almost impenetrable. Yet, in this book, Pepe make it very penetrable and fascinating. At the end of the book you feel like you can understand much of how it works so well that you almost feel quite an expert on the subject.

Pepe has an amazing way of making everything sound fun and enjoyable when he speaks and writes. For much of what is involved in research and marketing this isn't totally surprising, because it is a very fun and enjoyable world. However, the term 'neuroscience' sounds serious, difficult to come to terms with, something that perhaps it would be better to leave other people to work on and understand. But, in this book, neuroscience is described in layman's terms... and makes sense! So, if you are interested in knowing why consumers do what they do or indeed why you do what you do, this book helps to give a good idea of the different processes that go on in all our minds.

Catherine Kohler
Account Director
Firefly Millward Brown
Barcelona, Spain

ACKNOWLEDGEMENTS

First of all, I would like to dedicate this book to my wife Elena and my children, David and Patricia, because they are the three people who occupy the most important part of my mind. And I would like to thank my parents, brothers and sisters, for the very special imprint they have left on me. I have been lucky enough to receive the positive influence and values of a large family.

I would also like to give a mention here to all my family, friends, colleagues and customers. My mind is being shaped every day, and continues to be shaped thanks to my interactions with all these people.

I would like to give special thanks to the daily support I receive from Juan Ferrer-Vidal, Paul William Turner, Adolfo Fernández, Manuel Ameijeiras, Pilar Pérez, João Marques, María José Cañete, Reyes Neira, Beatriz Ozores and all those people working for Millward Brown Iberia.

Nigel Hollis, Gordon Pincott, Graham Page, Krzysztof Kruszewski, Pawel Ciacek and Cécile Conaré really helped me right from the start, when this book was a mere idea. I am very grateful for their patient reading of the manuscript, for all their helpful comments and for their welcoming words in the Preface.

Nigel Hollis and Gordon Pincott offered me their new brand analysis model ('Value Drivers Model'), which I have talked about in the chapter 'Brands, communications and the mind'.

Peter Walshe and Cristiana Pearson allowed me access to all their data from their research into 'The 100 most valuable global brands in 2010'. I would like to take this opportunity to thank them for the great work they have done.

With Vicente Condes I have enjoyed a rewarding working relationship and a good friendship. I would like to thank him for all those times when we put our heads together to think and reflect. He really helped me in turning this book into reality. He also added his contribution to the Preface.

The same goes for Enrique Larumbe. We have a professional mutual understanding and outside the working environment we share great personal chemistry. We haven't known each other for long, but we have succeeded in significant achievements. These have been both fruitful and fun. Thank you Enrique for your words here in this Preface.

I would like to thank the companies that appear in the book for their permission to include their studies on brand logos and advertising campaigns.

I would like to highlight the invaluable collaboration of Miquet Humphryes and Delyth Hughes, who took on the responsibility for resolving any logistical issues relating to the publication of this book (the manuscript, translation, editorial management, etc) so efficiently.

Also deserving of mention is the work of Jon Finch, Editorial Director at Kogan Page, who showed great interest in this book from the beginning.

And finally, I would like to thank Dani González for his collaboration and creativity. He created the graphics that appear throughout this book.

And last but not least I would also like to thank my colleague Catherine Kohler, from Firefly Millward Brown in Barcelona, for her attentive reading of the manuscript and for her kind words in the Preface.

And to all of you, my readers, many thanks for being here and being part of my life.

Pepe Martínez
Managing Director, Millward Brown Iberia

Introduction

The mind is not a vessel to be filled but a fire to be kindled.

PLUTARCH

A look back

As the history of thought has progressed, the human mind has suffered three major blows:

1 The first came during the Renaissance, when Nicolaus Copernicus stated that the Earth was not the centre of the universe. In those days it took a brave man to proclaim such a discovery: men had been sent to the gallows for less. In the new Copernican view of the cosmos the Earth shifted from its central position and was no longer the belly-button of the universe.

2 The 19th century saw the second blow, this time to human pride in its own existence. Charles Darwin was developing his theory of evolution, with all the consequences that this entailed: humans were no longer the ultimate aim of God's creation.

3 Then, towards the end of the 19th century and the start of the 20th, Sigmund Freud was responsible for landing the final blow (so far) with his view of the self and the environment surrounding humans. Freud highlighted the fact that humans are not completely rational beings. He showed how our behaviour is largely determined by subconscious elements and emotions.

The birth of neuroscience

Not long afterwards, towards the end of the 20th century, neuroscience was born. Daniel Goleman's book *Emotional Intelligence* was a major advance in this field. Antonio Damasio had already made the definitive step towards making this discipline relevant. His two major works, *Descartes' Error* and

Looking for Spinoza, are widely published and continue to have had a major impact. Neuroscience has highlighted the importance of emotions in the decision-making process. Damasio's concept of a 'somatic marker' has shown the influence of the subconscious aspects of our behaviour.

New technology allows us to study the brain and mind as it carries out its functions. In the 20th century the great Russian neuropsychologist, Alexander Luria, wrote a very interesting book, *The Working Brain*. The title was promising, but in those days the brain and mind could not be researched in the way they can today. During the 21st century we will be able to research the working brain with increasing accuracy. Modern technology is showing us the secrets of the brain and mind. This is going to be the century of the brain.

The brain is amazing. It is the only organ in the human body capable of thinking for itself. And all this thanks to neurones. The human brain is made up of 100,000 million neurones interconnected in complex ways.

Brain activity involves real teamwork – and that is not easy. Think of a football team, carrying out a university assignment, how a corporate department works, or the relationship between the different departments within a company. It's not easy is it? Well, in the case of the human brain this group activity extends to 100,000 million members: 100,000 million units working as a whole. Impressive!

José Antonio Marina, in his latest book, *El cerebro infantil: una gran oportunidad* (The infant brain: a great opportunity), says in the Introduction:

> The brain is a small continent – it weighs less than 1.5 kilogrammes – but it holds the greatest complexities of the universe. It makes up 2% of the weight of a human body, but it uses 20% of its energy, channelled through the 36 litres of blood it receives every hour.
>
> Everything about it is overwhelming. It is made up of a hundred thousand million neurones and over a billion glial cells, and we scarcely know how these function. Marian Diamond, of the University of California, discovered that the left parietal lobe of Einstein's brain had 77% more glial cells per neurone than other males of the same age, but we still don't know what this means.
>
> Every neurone can have thousands of links – some like the Purkinje cells in the cerebellum, up to 500,000 – which creates a total sum of a hundred billion approximately, because no one, obviously, has counted them one by one.
>
> Neurones are connected by almost one million six hundred thousand kilometres of nerve fibres. We have two hemispheres connected by the corpus callosum, a mass of two hundred million nerve fibres.
>
> The brain is constantly working, and specialists think that it can process up to 10 to the power of 27 bits per second, that is a one followed by twenty-seven zeros.
>
> They have discovered a 'default neural network', which works frenziedly while the brain is resting, that is to say when it appears to be doing nothing. And we can continue with this catalogue of heroic deeds.

This complex 'network' holds our entire life, our 'self', our personalities, our desires, our fears, our beliefs, our preconceptions, our vision of the future.

Our unique and unrepeatable self, our identity is to be found in the neurone circuits in our brain, in the synaptic connections that are created between these neurones throughout our life. In reality, we are the neuronal map or outline that is configured in our brains as the years go by.

Life's experiences and what we learn from life encourage the creation of neuronal networks and make it difficult, or impede, the formation of others. For this reason, we tend to rely on the strongest circuits, the ones we can control the best. We tend towards repetition.

We have to develop our mind, to show it new pathways, to develop new connections between neurones. As Albert Einstein said: 'If you want different results, do things differently.'

What is neuromarketing?

This is all well and good, but what is neuromarketing? It is the result of integrating three different disciplines:

1 *neurology*, which focuses on studying the human brain;
2 *cognitive psychology*, which studies the relationship between the human mind and behaviour; and
3 *marketing*, a term that has recently suffered from negative connotations, but is the discipline (a mix of science and art) that is responsible for developing new concepts for products and services that satisfy the needs of consumers/customers and, at the same time, are profitable.

Neuromarketing provides us with valuable help in furthering our understanding of:

● brand functioning;
● the effectiveness of communications;
● consumer behaviour; and
● the decision-making process when choosing purchases.

As such, neuromarketing is a very useful tool for drafting more effective strategies and plans of action for brands, communications and corresponding business plans.

We have come across three core attitude types to this new discipline of neuromarketing. Broadly speaking, these are the same ones we find whenever something new appears on the market: radicals, sceptics and admirers.

At one extreme we find the 'radicals' or extreme defenders, for whom neuromarketing is the new panacea, the new Holy Grail. These people are very critical about market research and consider neuromarketing is going to completely replace it.

Obviously, neuroscience is going to shed a lot of light on how the minds of consumers work through precise and objective measurements. For the moment it is a budding science. It will take a long time before it replaces traditional market research (if it ever does); for now it is an interesting and promising complement. However, adopting an extremist attitude is not appropriate.

At the other end of the spectrum are the 'sceptics' who look askance at any new ideas. They will not consider anything innovative until it has been firmly established. They always emphasize the problems; in this case, they tend to focus on the ethical problems, since we are talking about being in people's brains/minds. They see this discipline as a way of manipulating consumers.

Occupying the intermediate ground are the 'admirers' who tend towards a realistic optimism. Their minds are open to new ideas and to incorporating new methods into current tools. They would consider neuromarketing as a good, complementary addition to market research methods. It involves a new type of information because it is not declarative; it does not require 'feedback' from the consumer. This is a very interesting new development, because people are not aware of everything that goes on in their mind.

I consider myself to be part of this latter group, because the 'radicals' show an extreme attitude and 'sceptics' reject what market research brings to the table (consumers' statements are still important). Figure 1.1 shows these three attitudes.

FIGURE 1.1 Three core attitudes to this new discipline of neuromarketing

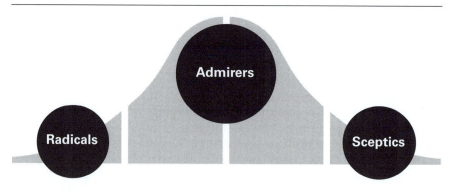

FIGURE 1.2 Four dimensions can be differentiated within the consumer mind

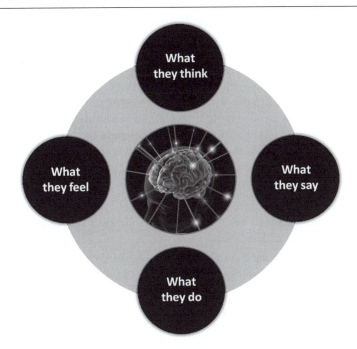

Four dimensions can be differentiated within the consumer mind, as shown in Figure 1.2:

What they think	→ the thought level	→ the cognitive model.
What they feel	→ the feelings level	→ the emotional model.
What they say	→ the spoken discourse (communicating, listening, speaking).	→ the language model
What they do	→ the behaviour level	→ the action level.

In traditional research (qualitative and quantitative) of an explicit nature, we have to work with what the consumer tells us: their verbal statements. At this point thoughts, feelings and behaviour are inferred. Some critics emphasize the fact that consumers contradict themselves, saying what they think, but doing what they feel. Researchers already know this, because we work with consumers on a daily basis. Our job is to analyse what they say, to identify the most important and relevant information, and interpret it for any inconsistencies we find.

With the arrival of ethnographical methods we had the opportunity to round out consumers' statements by observing their behaviour in their 'natural habitat'. This allowed us to compare and contrast their verbal discourse with their behaviour as they were shopping or using consumer products.

Neuroscience now offers us the possibility of directly recording consumers' thoughts and emotions. Therefore, it is an implicit research method (undeclared). This new information completes the explicit data – what consumers do and what they say.

The realities of the market and consumer phenomena are very complex. There are a lot of variables interacting at the same time. Qualitative and quantitative methods manage to capture a large part of the psycho-sociological phenomena in play, but there are some 'blind spots' that cannot be recorded. Combining the three methods (qualitative, quantitative and neuroscience) allows us to obtain a much richer snapshot of the market:

- The *qualitative* data gives us the richness of free discourse, shows the emergence of the most important aspects and gives a profound knowledge through interpretation.

- The *quantitative* data provides the security offered by statistics, precise mathematical measurements, the objectivity of quantities and representation through the concept of extension.

- Finally, *neuroscience* rounds out the previous methodologies because of its objectivity through the use of physiological measurements, the use of implicit modern technology and the ability to effectively sift through people's statements.

Figure 1.3 shows how these three methods complement each other.

FIGURE 1.3

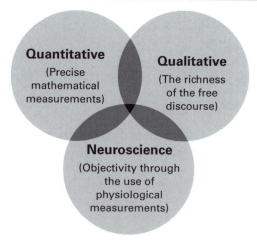

Neuroscience is already producing results

At Millward Brown we have already carried out several studies with various partners. We have worked with some top notch clients (manufacturers and service companies), with the academic world and with suppliers of technical equipment.

We have worked with electroencephalograms (brainwaves measurements, EEG). It is a very modern, functional and simple technology. It consists of fitting a comfortable band around the consumer's head and registering the brain's electrical activities whilst watching a stimulus (for example, a TV advertisement).

We have also used eye-tracking, which externally looks very similar to a computer screen, and is used to determine where the consumer's visual attention is focused when looking at a stimulus. Using these methods we have analysed numerous stimuli (logos, picture ads in magazines and billboards, packaging, shelving displays in shops, web pages, etc). We now have eye-tracking equipment available in many of Millward Brown's offices, throughout the world.

A glimpse of the future

The 21st century is going to be the century of the brain. Technology will continue its unstoppable advance and will allow us to follow the imprint left by communications, consumption and brand phenomena in consumers' minds.

This is going to change the way markets are researched and researchers' activities. At the moment we are only at the beginning of this new route and we have to be both modest and optimistic about the results we achieve. At the same time, ethical standards are being developed to guarantee the confidentiality of information from consumers. Any advance means new opportunities, but it also brings with it possible threats.

Everything hangs on the intentions behind using these new discoveries. The key is almost always the intention and significance of the actions carried out by the subject or organization using these technologies. It will be necessary to regulate the use of these new technologies to safeguard consumers' dignity and to protect them from any type of manipulation that could be related to purchasing and consuming products.

The aim of this book

The main aim is to take an amazing journey into the human mind. We are going to combine two perspectives in analysing our minds. At times we will look within ourselves as consumers and sometimes as people.

This is why this book has a twin approach. On the one hand, we offer a view of the consumer mind for all those professionals who work in the field of marketing or related areas, such as market research, advertising, media, sales departments, etc. In this same vein, the book is also suitable for students who are attracted to these professions (business school students, university alumni, etc). The aim is to penetrate consumers' minds, to gain a better understanding of their behaviour and to be able to predict, as far as possible, their future purchasing decisions.

This book is also for all those people who want to understand themselves better and to know a little bit more about how their minds and those of others work during their daily activities and interrelations that make up their life. Therefore, we shall delve into our mental functions as human beings and as individuals.

The vista we are going to provide is quite separate from the medicine, neurology, anatomy and physiology of the brain. We will offer a brief outline of neuroscience for a better understanding of the neural basis behind consumers' mental functions. Because within that mind are recorded the most successful brands and communications – unlike those that did not make it, those that went completely unnoticed.

Starting point: the pillars of the human mind

02

Each man can be, if he so determines, the sculptor of his own brain. **SANTIAGO RAMÓN Y CAJAL**

Evolution is capricious

The brain and the mind are inextricably intertwined. The brain corresponds to the bodily level, whilst the mind is on a higher plane. The brain is an organ; it is associated with biology, physiology and neurology. The mind is a function; it is associated with psychology, sociology, history and philosophy. If we compare it to computing, we can say that the brain is the hardware, whilst the mind is the software (the operating system).

In the beginning the human brain was not designed as it is now. It is the result of millions of years of evolution. There have been constant improvements on the initial results. The brain could be compared to a house. The house starts off small, and extends as it adapts to the growing needs of the people who live inside it. They have work done, they remodel, they make changes, and they build extensions. We also have to believe that our brains as they are now are not the end point. They are part of an evolutionary process. The brains of future generations will have new mental developments.

Our brain is a very complex, advanced and fascinating organ. The fact that it has undergone various evolutionary incarnations creates some difficulties with integrating its various parts; sometimes we even find faults in the system. For this reason it is very important to know about its structure and function, as this gives us a better understanding of the reactions, emotions, thoughts, discourse, etc of consumers (and of ourselves).

The triune brain

Overall, we can sum up the evolution of the human brain as the consecutive process of integrating three different animal species: reptiles, mammals and finally, human beings.

FIGURE 2.1

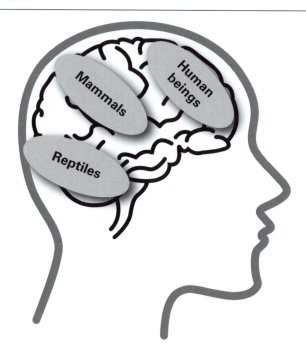

From reptiles we inherited the most basic and primitive part of the brain. This is our instinct function, and it works very well. The ultimate aim is survival. This part of the brain is responsible for regulating the homeostatic balance, reflexes, reproduction, automatic and programmed behaviour (routines, habits, territoriality, defending our living space), etc. Most of this type of behaviour is geared towards satisfying biological needs and defending against other animals.

Species with this type of brain focus on the present and on action. This means very simple and basic reactions: fight or flight (the biological response of animals to acute stress). There are still some humans who function according to this type of model, for example the psychopath, whose behaviour is very aggressive, predatory and without feeling – he or she feels no empathy with the victim; and the paranoiac, who always sees him or herself as the victim, and sees dangers and threats everywhere.

As mammals began to appear on the evolutionary timeline, they incorporated new brain structures. The limbic system, also known as the 'emotional brain', makes its appearance. Mammals now have motivation, restraint, desires, emotions and basic feelings. Along with these, the ability to learn becomes part of the memory. For this reason, concepts such as 'the present' and 'action' that we see in reptiles, the ideas of the 'past' and 'emotion' as contributed by mammals must now be added. From a psychopathological point of view, there are known and widespread neuroses. In these cases, an emotional trauma has occurred that has not been properly linked to the corresponding ideas, which means the person suppresses them in his or her unconscious.

The last stage in the brain's development occurred with the arrival of more highly evolved mammals including primates and some cetaceans. This produced a major development of the neocortex (cerebral cortex), which is a fine layer covering practically the whole brain. This evolutionary leap forward allowed the function of thought to be incorporated and humans now had the ability to think of a future. This completes the current mental apparatus:

reptiles	+	mammals	+	human beings
act	+	feel	+	think
past	+	present	+	future

Wikipedia summarizes the current view on this model:

The triune brain is a model of the evolution of the vertebrate forebrain and behavior proposed by the American physician and neuroscientist Paul D MacLean. He originally formulated his model in the 1960s and propounded it at length in his 1990 book *The Triune Brain in Evolution*.

MacLean's recognition of the limbic system as a major functional system in the brain has won wide acceptance among neuroscientists, and is generally regarded as his most important contribution to the field.

The triune brain idea holds little in favour in current neuroscience. Subsequent findings have invalidated the traditional neuroanatomical ideas upon which MacLean based his hypothesis, although the three functional domains described by the original triune model remain useful organizing themes and concepts.

The triune model continues to hold interest for some psychologists and members of the general public because of its focus on the recognizable differences between most reptiles, early mammals, and late mammals. Reasons for the success are its simplicity; the theory in this form recognizes three major evolutionary periods in the development of the brain that are characterized by three recognizably distinct ways of solving adaptive challenges.

The popularity of the model can also be seen in the way it parallels recurring themes in popular culture and the arts. For example, some languages have phrases which refer to speaking from the 'head', 'heart' or 'gut', or philosophically of the three virtues of 'wisdom, benevolence and courage', or psychologically of 'thinking', 'feeling' and 'willing'.

Table 2.1 shows a comparison of these three levels.

TABLE 2.1

Reptiles	**Gut**	**Courage**	**Willing**	**Act**
Mammals	**Heart**	**Benevolence**	**Feeling**	**Feel**
Human beings	**Head**	**Wisdom**	**Thinking**	**Think**

The four basic mental functions

If we focus more specifically on human beings, there are three differentiating characteristics:

1 the major development of the frontal lobe (prefrontal cortex);
2 the ability to use language and communicate; and
3 the perception of awareness (consciousness).

There are other aspects that have also been crucial in the development of humans and their culture. For example, the way the thumb is positioned in a human hand has allowed us to make tools and manipulate objects; being able to control fire has meant that we can cook food and given us access to different food sources.

As a result of this long evolutionary process, our current brains project upwards from the back of the neck, towards the forehead, in a treelike structure. At neck level, the nervous system hides its roots within the body by packing them into the spinal cord. This bundle of nerves relays communications between the head and the rest of the body. In brief, there are three levels within the structure of our brain:

1 The first is made up of the brainstem and the cerebellum (little brain). This is the lower part of the brain. It is the most primitive and basic part. It is responsible for supplying energy to the body, for homeostatic regulation, for controlling automatic behaviour and for motor activity. It is like the maintenance area in an apartment block. This level is related to the present and to action.

2 The second level is the intermediate area of the brain, the core as it were. This is the limbic system. It has a circular form – the word 'limbic' comes from the Latin *limbus* meaning ring. It incorporates

learning from the past, memory and emotions. There are four important structures that are referred to throughout the rest of the book: the thalamus, the hypothalamus, the amygdala and the hippocampus. As this area is concerned with emotions, it can become a real pressure cooker. It is a 'hot' area.

3 Finally, we reach the most evolved area of the brain: the cerebral cortex, and especially the frontal lobe. This is where the rational level comes into play (thought, reasoning, decision-making, etc) and planning for the future. The prefrontal cortex is the control tower, the directional system for the brain and mind. It is a 'cold' area and the one that does the calculating.

I would like to make it clear that this approach is a simplification and is just a way of illustrating it. These three levels are very closely interrelated. Everything is connected to everything else. In reality, this entity that we know as the 'self', that observer of external reality and the internal world is a complex integration of body, brain and mind. For example, the emotions have their origin in the limbic system but are 'felt' in the prefrontal cortex and become manifest on a physical level.

To the three previous levels, corresponding to doing, feeling and thinking, we now add a fourth level, communication, or language: the act of saying things to others and listening to them. All four levels are shown in Figure 2.2.

FIGURE 2.2 The four basic mental functions

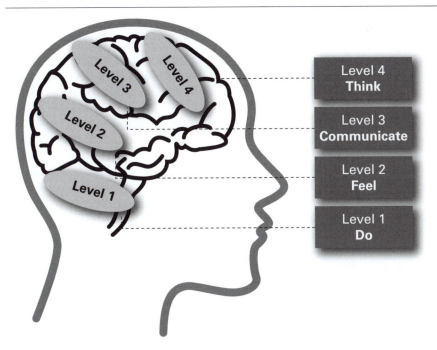

Level 3

Level 4

Level 2

Level 1

| Level 4 |
| **Think** |

| Level 3 |
| **Communicate** |

| Level 2 |
| **Feel** |

| Level 1 |
| **Do** |

It is important to analyse the level of integration of these four functions within a single person. There are people who think a lot, sometimes even too much, but they find it difficult to turn these thoughts into actions. They spend their lives thinking but never do anything about it. Every specific case is its own world. Equally, there are minds that are always acting, usually impulsively, because they are incapable of stopping to think about the consequences of their actions. Emotions push them towards actions and they cannot relate this to the thought area. And of course, there are many combinations of the two.

Do we make sufficient use of these four areas of mental activity? Is there any consistency between what we do, feel, say and think? These four mental function indicators are the key to analysing the way a person behaves (in their personal or professional life), in the way a consumer behaves, or how a brand behaves within its established category.

Is our brand consistent? Is there any synchronization between what we do, feel, say and think? This is the key to its credibility. These days consumers are very sensitive to brand authenticity. If a brand is not credible, its rhetoric will fail and its competitiveness will decrease significantly.

When qualitative market research users attend group meetings to monitor events, they sometimes comment that consumers contradict themselves between their individual and social discourses. Clearly they contradict themselves because their minds have different levels, and functions that are not properly integrated. The mind does what it can. Consumers are not logic-based, mathematical computers, fortunately! This is why the researcher, who understands the various dimensions in which the mind of the consumer moves, has to analyse and interpret consumer discourse.

For example, consumers usually say what they think but do what they feel. If there are some contradictions in the consumers' discourse, researchers try to shift the focus onto what they do (their behaviour) and what they feel (their emotions). A teenage girl who is really keen on a boy in her class may be significantly influenced by what the boy says, but she may be confused. He might tell her he really loves her, but largely ignores her. When things are not clear, it is better to be guided by the behaviour and emotions that someone demonstrates and not so much by their words. Words sometimes drift away on the breeze.

We have to exercise these four mental functions. If we are not aware of our emotions, we live in a state of neurosis, and feelings could pop up at any time in our lives, giving us a huge shock. If emotions are unable to surface normally, they will find another outlet.

If the area of thought and language takes no notice of the emotional brain, these emotions cannot come to the surface (rational world), so they are buried within the body itself, and they begin to deposit this energy at the biological level (in the stomach, heart, skin, etc). These are what we know as psychosomatic disorders.

The greater the level of integration between these four areas, the more genuine we will be, happier in ourselves and we will have much more satisfying relationships with others. Our mind is the result of having evolved through different stages. It has gradually incorporated functions. It needs integration and synchronization. This way it works best and most effectively.

The mind and the theatre

Our minds are very complex. The mind could be compared to a theatre production. (I haven't gone mad! Or at least I don't think so.)

In our daily lives there is a feeling that there are several characters at work within our mind. Obviously these are integrated and we feel like one entity with one identity. Yet, at the same time, it is as if we were having a dialogue with ourselves.

It is important to identify the characters acting in our daily theatre production. Sometimes there is one who is very disciplined, urging us to behave in a thoroughly responsible manner. At other times, another character who is very impulsive pops up and insists that we give in to our desires and emotions. It is not unusual for there to be a struggle between these various characters, at different times of the day as well as during various stages in life.

The characters affecting our minds are quite diverse and they vary greatly from one person's mind to another. These characters and their corresponding 'roles' are shaped in infancy and evolve throughout our lives, depending on how we treat them and how we work with them on a daily basis.

There are characters that slip our control; this can endanger our relationship with ourselves and with others. In the most extreme cases, when these characters gain complete autonomy, the mind strays into the area of psychopathology. With very serious diseases, such as major psychoses, these characters take on their own lives and manifest themselves as people giving orders to the subject (hearing voices, feeling compelled to behave in a certain way and so on).

But, let's not be overdramatic: this only occurs in very special circumstances. It is unusual for the mind to go so far. What we usually feel is that our mind is working as a team, with the frontal lobe taking the lead, but having to negotiate with the rest of the brain, rather like the board of directors in a company. In life, you can only succeed as part of a team. It is very difficult to achieve goals absolutely independently.

Enter your mind!

What do we currently know about the brain? In this section we are going to take a fascinating journey into the depths of the mind. So, fasten your seat belts.

FIGURE 2.3

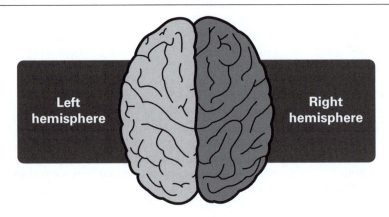

The brain consists of two cerebral hemispheres, joined internally by a structure known as the *corpus callosum*. Each one has a slight specialization. This is very common in cerebral function: some areas take the lead in certain specific functions. But that is all it is – taking the lead – because the brain and mind work as a team. As Antonio Damasio describes in his book, *Looking for Spinoza*, 'the mind as emerges from the cooperation of many brain regions'.

The left hemisphere is also known as the language and logic brain. In most people it assumes greater responsibility for the following functions:

- language (spoken and written);
- logical reasoning;
- numeracy skills; and
- controlling the right side of the body.

The right hemisphere is also known as the emotional and spatial brain. In most individuals it assumes greater responsibility for the following functions:

- the emotional world;
- imagination, creativity and artistic skills;
- spatial perception; and
- controlling the left side of the body.

We have to be very careful with the functions we assign each hemisphere. Every day more research is undertaken into this subject, and there are aspects that are still not clear. Wikipedia alerts us to this point:

> The concept of right brain and left brain thinking developed from the research in the late 1960s of an American psychobiologist Roger W Sperry. He discovered that the human brain has two very different ways of thinking. One (the right brain) is visual and processes information in an intuitive and simultaneous way,

looking first at the whole picture then the details. The other (the left brain) is verbal and processes information in an analytical and sequential way, looking first at the pieces then putting them together to get the whole. Sperry was awarded a Nobel Prize in 1981, although subsequent research has shown things aren't quite as polarized as once thought (nor as simple).

Broad generalizations are often made in popular psychology about certain functions (eg logic, creativity) being lateralized, that is, located in the right or left side of the brain. These ideas need to be treated carefully because the popular lateralizations are often distributed across both sides.

There is some evidence that the right hemisphere is more involved in processing novel situations, while the left hemisphere is most involved when routine or well-rehearsed processing is called for.

Other integrative functions, including arithmetic, binaural sound localization, and emotions (lateralization of emotion), seem more bilaterally controlled.

Left hemisphere functions: numerical computation (exact calculation), direct fact retrieval and language (grammar/vocabulary, literal). Right hemisphere functions: numerical computation (approximate calculation) and language (intonation/accentuation, prosody, pragmatic, contextual). Terence Hines states that the research on brain lateralization is valid as a research exercise, although commercial organizations have applied it to promote subjects and products far outside the implications of the research.

The human brain is divided into two hemispheres – left and right. Scientists continue to explore how some cognitive functions tend to be dominated by one side or the other, that is, how they are lateralized.

We have to be very cautious about the function of the brain's hemispheres, because we often attribute activities to one of the hemispheres while they are actually the result of real teamwork.

The cerebral cortex, the most advanced and evolved part of our brain, is divided into four lobes, as shown in Figure 2.4. The mind's abilities, so advanced and complex, are closely related to this part of the brain.

The figure shows us the four lobes that make up the brain, plus the cerebellum. The occipital lobe, located in the area of the head we call the nape of the neck, is completely dedicated to visual perception, the most complex of our senses.

The parietal lobe is in the uppermost part of the head. The left-hand side is dedicated to making calculations, writing and collaborating in the body's movements. The right-hand side works on activities involving spatial dimensions (turning objects in the mind, 3-D and dimensionality), recognizing faces and drawing.

The temporal lobe is directly under the parietal lobe, above the ears. The left-hand side specializes in language, whilst the right-hand side collaborates in the perception function.

Finally, there is the frontal lobe, located above the eyes, behind the forehead (which is where the name comes from). It is the most recent part added by the evolutionary process and offers us the latest generation in brains.

FIGURE 2.4

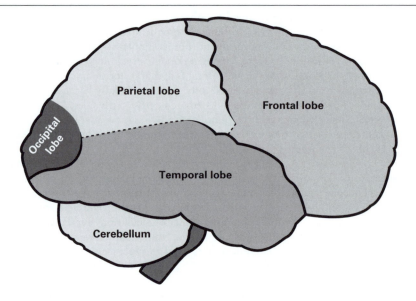

Human beings are not fitted with standard equipment. Facilities have been added as new requirements have emerged. The frontal lobe carries out very high level mental functions:

- reasoning and thinking;
- future planning;
- it is the management and executive area in a human;
- it is directly involved in problem solving;
- intelligence;
- consciousness;
- the concept of 'self';
- personality;
- the social dimension;
- ethical and moral judgements (conscience).

As we shall see in the chapters on emotions and decision making, the frontal lobe plays a key role in coordinating thoughts and feelings. The right-hand side registers negative feelings, such as fear and aggression. This area is known as the discomfort centre. The left-hand side houses the switch that regulates negative experiences and is the centre for well-being.

The frontal lobe also has a very active role in the attention process and the functions of operational memory. These functions allow the brain to work on external information or information that is stored in internal reality.

The frontal lobe does not hold any information; instead its capability consists of acting the best way possible on the information available. It has two parts: the dorsolateral nuclei (behind the temples) and the ventro-medial areas (the lower and central parts of the lobe).

Having briefly described the rudiments of the human brain and mind, we are now ready to delve deeper to reveal its mysteries.

Summary of key learning points about brands

- Brands have to be coherent and genuine to be credible. There has to be a relationship between what they think (their values), the emotions they convey and create (what they feel), what they say (their communications) and the actions they carry out (what they do).

- A brand's credibility is essential to attracting consumers and earning their loyalty.

- A brand's coherence must be obvious in all levels of the marketing mix: concept, product, image, communications, packaging-labelling, advertising, varieties of the product, distribution and price.

- Danone is a manufacturer of dairy products. The essence of this brand is the concepts of health, enjoyment (products that are pleasurable to eat) and the idea of modernity (products that are functional, individual and fast). Danone sells brand-name products like Activia (to aid the digestive function), Actimel (to strengthen the body's defences), Danacol (to reduce cholesterol), and Densia (for bones). If an umbrella brand like Danone positions itself to focus on health, enjoyment and modernity, all the elements that make up each of its brands and their strategies have to be coherent and convey this positioning.

The alarm clock rings

03

"To my mind the human brain is the most marvellous and mysterious object in the whole universe.

HENRY FAIRFIELD OSBORN

Think of a typical working day. For example, it is a Wednesday, midway through the week. The hands of the clock move to 7.30 and the alarm bell rings. Our brain suddenly receives the clock's alarm signal. In the dark, we slowly reach out a hand to stop the ringing. The first thought of the day comes into your mind: 'How awful, it's Wednesday, I have to go to work.' We languish between the sheets.

When the alarm clock rings our brain switches from 'off' to 'on'. The mind has a device similar to a light switch. The brain lights up when it hears the alarm clock on the bedside table, rather like a dimmer switch that gradually increases the intensity of the lighting in a room.

The reticular formation, also known as the reticular activating system, is the mind's alarm clock. While it is switched off the person is asleep. When it switches on it sends signals to the whole brain. It is called 'reticular' because it has a type of network structure spread throughout the brain. The reticular formation is found at level 1, in the subcortical structures of the brain, in the brainstem, as shown in Figure 3.1.

When it is switched on it maintains the brain in a state of mental alertness (arousal). If the reticular formation receives very intense stimulation, the person enters a state of stress. If its activation gradually decreases the person slips into a state of drowsiness. When it reaches the 'off' position, the brain sleeps.

The noun 'arousal' and its verb 'to arouse' mean to wake up, to stimulate. Arousal is the activation level for the nervous system, on both the physiological and psychological planes. It tells us to what extent we are awake and how we react to the stimuli that reach us from the external world and from within our own bodies.

Hans Eysenck (1916–1997), the German behavioural psychologist, distinguished between various types of people. Among them are extrovert

FIGURE 3.1 The reticular formation

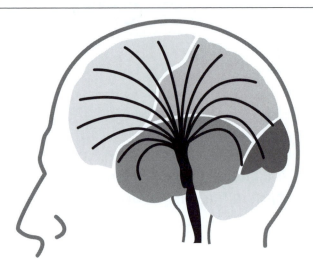

and introvert personalities. For this researcher extrovert individuals have a low level of arousal, so they look for a strong relationship with their environment; they are hungry for stimuli. Introverted people have a high level of cerebral activity, so they do not need such active exchanges with other people.

I have already mentioned José Antonio Marina's book *El cerebro infantil: una gran oportunidad* (The infant brain: a great opportunity); he also discusses Eysenck:

> I am particularly interested in Eysenck's theories on the temperament and his rigorous biological approaches and because they have a significant educational application. He distinguished two behavioural dimensions to which we all belong:
>
> Introversion   –   Extroversion
> Emotional stability   –   Emotional instability

The introvert-extrovert dimension includes differences in sociability and impulsiveness. The typical extrovert is sociable, they like parties, they have a lot of friends, they need excitement and they act impulsively. The introvert tends to be calm, introspective, reserved, reflective, suspicious of impulsive decisions and prefers a well-ordered life to one full of chance and risk.

The most interesting part is the explanation offered by Eysenck. He believes that we all have an optimum level of activation/excitation/stress that we feel comfortable with. If it is too low we become bored, and if it is too high we feel anxious.

For introverts this level of activation is very high, so any additional stimulus could surpass the limit of what they can tolerate and cause anxiety. This is why they tend to look for less exiting environments. It is obvious that they can have an extraordinarily intense and creative life, but in a calm environment.

On the other hand, extroverts have a very low level of activity and so they need to be continuously looking for external stimuli, emotions and very animated environments. Otherwise, they become bored.

The second dimension is between the unstable emotions (neuroticism in Eysenck's terminology) and stable emotions. Those who complain about their worries and their anxiety, as well as their physical pain, headaches, stomach problems and vertigo.

In those first moments of the day, once we have got out of bed, a whole series of automatic behaviours are triggered that do not require conscious intervention. We switch off the alarm clock, put on our slippers, and head towards the bathroom, we take a shower, eat our breakfast, brush our teeth, etc.

These automatic behaviours do not require the participation of higher mental processes. You don't need to think to do them. This means an important energy saving for the brain. The thought process delegates these actions to the basic cerebral structures.

These habits and ritual behaviours are ingrained in the way we function on a daily basis and are very difficult to change. Sometimes we think that, at that time in the morning, before we have that first cup of coffee, we are like 'zombies' or that we are on automatic pilot. Our behaviour is comparable to a robot. Since there is no directly conscious activity, we can be unsure about the actions we have just carried out, asking ourselves, for example, 'Did I close the car door when I parked this morning?' For obsessive minds these doubts can reach exceptional levels.

Throughout human evolution thought and language have taken control over movement. This is why we use the television remote control so we do not have to get up to change the channel. Neurons take direct action on the muscles. When this involves such a basic activity, so automatic, so repetitive ... the consciousness allows the body a certain level of autonomy.

Market products and brands stimulate consumers' senses (by how they look, smell, taste, touch, etc) and trigger positive feelings which lead to repetition. A brand's objective is to become part of consumer's buying and consumption rituals by generating a gratifying experience. This happens with the smell of a shampoo, the feel of a moisturizing cream, the smell and taste of coffee, the minty taste of toothpaste, the smell of our favourite cologne, etc.

It is very important for brands to achieve this integration into the consumer's daily, ritualistic behaviour. This generates a high level of dependency (loyalty) on behalf of the users. Consuming these products becomes a natural, integral part of our lives.

It is not just when we wake up that we carry out these automatic activities. We do so throughout the day: when we type using the computer keyboard; when we drive a car; when we ride a bicycle – and on many other occasions. It is strange that if we start to think about what we are doing it can be counterproductive: just by thinking about a process, the activity goes wrong. It is much better to delegate such activities to the motor system, which carries out orders automatically.

A few days ago I wanted to type an e-mail using my BlackBerry, but I could not remember the password. The more I thought about it, the less able I was to bring the password to mind. Then I decided just to let my fingers take control. Oddly enough they 'knew' the password. They had the information recorded in their movements. Our motor system can be more effective at carrying out some specific tasks by itself.

It is the brain's level 1 function that takes charge of coordinating these types of automatic movements where there is no need for conscious thought. Both the brainstem and the cerebellum work on carrying out these ritualistic movements correctly.

Other areas of the brain also take part; the main actors are the brainstem and cerebellum. We must always bear in mind that the activities carried out by our nervous system are very complicated and involve many parts working in conjunction with each other. Our brain and mind are the best examples of real teamwork.

Summary of key learning points about brands

- Market products and brands stimulate consumers' senses (through their look, smell, taste, touch, etc) and this triggers positive feelings that lead to repeat purchases (brand loyalty).

- A brand's objective is to become part of consumer's buying and consumption rituals by generating a gratifying experience. This happens with the fragrance of a shampoo, the feel of a moisturizing cream, the aroma of coffee, the minty taste of toothpaste, the smell of our favourite cologne, etc.

- It is very important for brands to integrate themselves in the consumer's daily, ritualistic behaviour. This generates a high level of dependency (loyalty) on behalf of the users. Consuming these products becomes a natural part of our lives.

The world surrounding us

04

One lives the idea, not the reality.   **ELEUTERIO MANERO**

External versus internal reality

From the very second we wake up external reality floods our minds through our five senses. We receive millions of stimuli throughout the day: the smell of a warming croissant in the corner café where we grab our usual morning coffee, the news on the car radio, the ad campaigns plastered all along the city's streets.

There are two information superhighways we all have between the 'real' external world (objective) and the internal, psychological world (subjective). The inbound information superhighway from external reality to the brain is the 'bottom-up' pathway, and the outbound superhighway, the person's response, is the 'top-down' pathway. Figure 4.1 shows us the two routes via which information circulates.

These two routes work in a complementary fashion. The first of these (bottom-up) comes from the outside world. As we stand in the supermarket aisle choosing a shower gel, there are a host of different products trying to tempt us to buy them. These products all vie for our attention through their packaging (shape, size, material, etc), the labelling (message, colours, images, etc) or because they conjure up a TV ad campaign.

All these stimuli reach us through the senses of sight and smell (often we open a bottle of fabric softener to smell its perfume). Sometimes touch also comes into play. Other times it is taste; for example if there is a tasting session for a new food product in the supermarket, there is usually a very nice, attractive young lady inviting us to try a morsel. Our body's senses do magic by transforming these senses (colours, sizes, shapes, smells, etc) into energy that can be processed (electric impulses, bits and bytes of information).

It is the bottom-up pathway that starts with stimuli from the outside world; these reach our senses, then perceptions, and finally they reach the

FIGURE 4.1

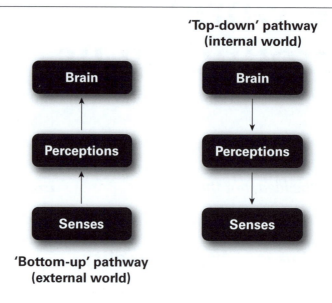

'Top-down' pathway
(internal world)

'Bottom-up' pathway
(external world)

higher structures of the brain responsible for processing and interpreting information received, decision making and ordering our motor system to buy the product we are thinking about and that will give us most satisfaction.

Our mind influences perception

The top-down pathway traces a trajectory in exactly the opposite direction. The two pathways travel almost in parallel. The top-down signals start in the person's mind, in the higher brain structures, where needs and desires are to be found. It is precisely because of these needs and desires (memory and emotions) that a person focuses his or her attention on specific stimuli; that is, the brain focuses its attention on that part of the external reality it thinks relevant. This pathway begins in the brain, focusing its attention, perceptions and senses in one direction. In these instances, a person's psychological reality is active and chooses between the many options offered by the external world. This is known as selective attention. Figure 4.2 illustrates this trajectory.

FIGURE 4.2 'Top-down' pathway (internal world)

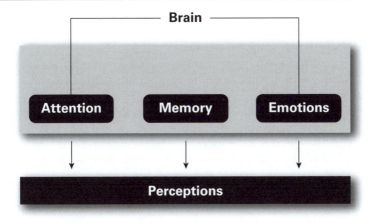

In August 2009, I travelled with my family to the west coast of the United States. In Los Angeles I went into a store and saw the red T-shirt that appears in Figure 4.3.

FIGURE 4.3

If we stay true to the information reaching us through our senses (bottom-up pathway) we should be reading two words in English that tell us how much we are enjoying California. But since learning, memory and emotions influence our perception (top-down pathway) we are probably decoding the message to say that we enjoy Coca-Cola.

These two perception highways are lively and dynamic. They are complementary. Both function at the same time, simultaneously. The traffic flows in both directions. On one side we have the external reality that reaches us through the senses and on the other we have the internal reality (the subjective dimension) that influences our perception of the world that surrounds us.

This dynamism between the external and the internal (the world and the mind), applied to the sense of sight, is expressed quite aptly in the famous phrase from the language expert and writer, Lin Yutang: 'Half of the beauty of a landscape depends on the region and the other half on the man looking at it.' Montaigne suspected there was a relationship between the two perception pathways. He expressed it in relation to the sense of sound: 'The word is half his that speaks, and half his that hears it.' José Antonio Marina also referred to the two perception highways (bottom-up and top-down) in his latest book. He says:

> Let's look at it from what we know. A good hunter sees tracks where the layman only sees earth. The same happens with all our sense registers. A cardiologist uses a stethoscope to listen for a series of sound patterns that will tell him whether that person's heart valves are working properly, for example. A wine expert recognizes the year and the region where the wine has been produced.
>
> In perception, as with so many other brain functions, two types of processes occur. One is the bottom-up process that builds information based on the senses, with the fine detail of a bricklayer. Each retinal receptor responds to a stimulus, the image reaches the eye, it is chopped into pieces and then rebuilt in the cortex of the occipital lobe.
>
> Our brain takes advantage of higher level information, saving it in our memory to round out the information received and to interpret it better. For example, when we do not understand a language, it requires a real effort on our part to distinguish where a word ends and another one begins. We hear an indiscernible, continuous sound. Conversely, when we understand it, we can do this without difficulty. Our brain tends to use the most detailed information whenever it can.

Let us now look at an example of how a logo is perceived.

The perception of the FedEx logo

According to Michael Evamy in his book *Logo*:

> Logos are signs, marks of identity designed for easy recognition. They are used by every kind of organization in every part of the world, from international corporations to charities and from political parties to community groups and schools. Logos also identify individual products and services ... logos operate on a sliding scale between the purely verbal and the purely visual.

Those logos that are part of the purely visual category, such as Apple, Nike or Vodafone, for example, do not need to write the name of the brand. They have reached the highest level of abstraction in the human mind so that just seeing the symbol brings to mind the brand: 'the logo is the focal point of any identity system and the key to its acceptance'. The logo is a key element to the brand but, 'It is the experience of individuals that gives a logo real associations and real meaning' (clients, consumers).

Have you heard of FedEx? Do you know which sector it operates in? It is part of the express delivery market and competes with SEUR, DHL, UPS and many other domestic and foreign companies.

FedEx is an air transport and logistics company, based in the United States, that covers an international market. It was founded under the name Federal Express in 1971 by Frederick W Smith in Little Rock (Arkansas). Later, in 1973, it moved to Memphis, Tennessee. Its current name and logo are an abbreviation of the company's original name: 'FedEx' is made up of the initial letters of the words 'Federal' and 'Express'. This is a very common way of creating names, taking part of each of the original names to make up a new configuration. The bank merger between BBV (Banco Bilbao Vizcaya) and Argentaria gave rise to its current name, BBVA. It is rather like the union between a man and a woman giving birth to a new life: a new-born baby.

Are you familiar with the logo for FedEx? You can see it in Figure 4.4.

FIGURE 4.4

When I was invited to lecture at various universities (Madrid, Barcelona, León, Oviedo, Pamplona, San Sebastián, Istanbul ...) I asked students to look at this logo and tell me where their attention was drawn (bottom-up route).

Almost all of them said that they were drawn to the central area where the letters 'd' and 'E' met. This is because of the contrasting colours. The letters 'F', 'e' and 'd' are purple, and the letters 'E' and 'x' are in orange. It is the most innovative and eye-catching part of the logo, because those two letters (the 'd' and the 'E') are joined together back-to-back. So, when we decode the brand 'FedEx' through the top-down pathway, we mainly focus on the central part, on the letters 'd' (in purple, lower case lettering) and 'E' (in orange, upper case lettering). This begins with the sense of sight, and then visual perception brings it to our attention and focuses on that part of the logo.

We can carry out experiments on a group of people using eye-tracking technology to check if what they say corresponds with the focus of their visual perception. Eye-tracking is an ultra-modern device for recording an individual's visual perception. By doing these experiments we can effectively check whether visual perception does go precisely to the part of the logo where the letters 'd' and 'E' meet, as shown in Figure 4.5.

FIGURE 4.5

I then tell the university students that there is something else they should see in the logo. Usually there is one student who says that he or she saw an arrow, amid the general shuffling and murmuring from the rest of the class. In Figure 4.6 the arrow is highlighted.

FIGURE 4.6

Then I tell them that there is indeed an arrow, and I prove it by highlighting it, as in Figure 4.6. The arrow was there before (in the external reality), but our mind did not see it. It has a very subtle presence – so subtle that most people do not see it. However, after they have been told about it, whenever the students see the image again they cannot help staring at the arrow. In fact, the first thing they see now is the arrow. Learnt information travels bottom-up, directly influencing the way the logo is perceived.

The eye-tracking equipment confirms what the students say, and how the process of perceiving external reality has evolved by using this logo. A learning process has occurred and their perception of the FedEx brand logo will never be the same.

Figure 4.7 shows us how the brain, now it knows about the arrow message, focuses its attention on this new area of the FedEx logo (top-down route).

FIGURE 4.7

Even if we go back to the original logo, the one I showed you in Figure 4.4, our visual attention still focuses on the arrow. First we see the arrow, and then we see the rest of the logo.

Analysis of different logos

Every logo has a history behind it and Michael Evamy had delved into the roots of many of these, as follows.

> The Kellogg's logo is a classic case of using the founder's signature as a guarantee of authenticity.

> There are many cases where a signature or a derivation of a signature is used, such as Disney and Johnson & Johnson.

> The first Apple logo, designed by the co-founder Ron Wayne, was a 'gothic' illustration of Isaac Newton sitting under an apple tree with a banner that read 'Apple Computer Inc.' Steve Jobs hired the young art director, Rob Janoff, to design a logo that could be reproduced more clearly. He began with the outline of an apple, but he thought it looked too much like a cherry tomato, so he added the bite taken out of one side to give an idea of the scale; 'bite' was also a play on words with 'byte'.

> 3M comes from the group's original name: Minnesota Mining & Manufacturing Company.

> In the Audi logo, 'the four rings symbolize the merger in 1932 of four independent automobile manufacturers: Audi, DKW, Horch and Wanderer.'

> Henri Nestlé was a Swiss pharmacist who developed an alternative source of nutrition for babies who could not tolerate their mother's milk. He adopted his own family crest as the logo for his company; in his German dialect, Nestlé means 'little nest'. The image of a bird feeding her chicks was 'unsurpassable'.

> As regards CNN, he says that: 'the channel needed a logo that would suggest an uninterrupted continuity, connections, refinement and power.'

The snaking letters, with the Ns close together in a wave pattern, as if it was a pulse, managed to convey this idea'.

Unilever: the new logo is a radical contrast to Unilever's old identity formed by a sterile 'U', in use since 1970. The new brand breathes the group's new mission: 'adding vitality to life'. The company launched a new logo that 'told the story of Unilever and its vitality'. It consists of 25 iconic illustrations representing Unilever and its brands: the spoon evokes the kitchen; the shirt, a washing line; a bee, hard work and biodiversity; and so on.

Amazon: 'everything from A to Z sent with a smile'.

Analysis of the Carrefour logo

Towards the end of 2009 I was giving a class at the University of Navarra in Pamplona. I was telling them about the case of the FedEx logo. Then one of the students mentioned that something similar happened with the Carrefour logo. I asked him to explain, and he said that the letter 'C' within the Carrefour logo was often not perceived by many people. I had to confess that I had not realized that there was a 'C' in the graphic of the Carrefour logo. I was really interested in this new case of logo perception.

The first thing we did was carry out market research on logos in general, and on the Carrefour logo in particular. The investigation was set up as follows:

- The sample consisted of members of the general public aged between 18 and 75.
- Area: Spain (Peninsula, Balearic Islands and Canary Islands).
- Technique: Computer Assisted Telephone Interviewing system (CATI).
- Sample: 1,000 interviews from the reference population.
- Sample design: representative of a national level by region and 'habitat', with quotas for sex, age and social class.
- Questionnaire: asked two completely spontaneous questions in October 2009.
- Fieldwork: all the interviews were carried out by a full-time team and an expert in telephone interviews from Millward Brown.

The question put to them was: 'I want you to think about brand logos. Can you tell me any that come to mind?' The interviewees began to search their long term memory (LTM) to see what they could find. Of the group interviewed, 70 per cent remembered at least one brand logo. The rest, 30 per cent, couldn't remember any.

Of the 700 people who mentioned a logo, the ones most frequently remembered were as follows:

- 27 per cent mentioned Coca-Cola;
- 7 per cent Nike;

- 4 per cent Telefónica and Adidas;
- 3 per cent Movistar and Danone;
- 2 per cent Carrefour, Renault, El Corte Inglés and Vodafone;
- 1 per cent BMW.

As you can see from the consumers' responses, the Carrefour logo cropped up spontaneously as one of those most remembered. This was good news, bearing in mind that this was a very open question (brand logos in general). In other words, the Carrefour logo is one of the best known and recognized among Spaniards.

Just a few weeks later, another sample of 1,000 people with the same characteristics as the previous sample were asked the following question: 'Think of supermarket logos. Can you tell me which ones come to mind?' The results were:

- 35 per cent said Carrefour;
- 14 per cent Eroski;
- 11 per cent Alcampo;
- 10 per cent Hipercor.

As you can clearly see, the Carrefour logo was the most remembered logo from among the supermarkets operating in Spain. The identity markers for Mercadona went unnoticed. The Mercadona logo is based mainly on lettering and does not have graphics; its identity was diluted in the memory of those taking part.

Next, the 354 people who spontaneously mentioned Carrefour were asked a second question: 'You told me you remembered the Carrefour logo; can you describe it to me?' We received the following replies:

- 37 per cent referred to the colour blue;
- 29 per cent made mention of the colour red;
- 18 per cent referred to a 'C';
- 15 per cent made a comment relating to the arrow;
- 10 per cent referred to the colour white;
- the rest of the answers were about circles, ovals, round shapes, the Carrefour name, the Carrefour name in red and blue, and geometric shapes.

So, the elements of the Carrefour logo that most grab consumers' attention are:

- the blue;
- the red;
- the 'C';
- the arrow; and
- the white.

Let's remind ourselves of the Carrefour logo.

FIGURE 4.8

We then decided to carry out more research using eye-tracking. We presented the Carrefour logo to a new sample of consumers, and we obtained the results shown in Figure 4.9.

FIGURE 4.9

The areas most of the consumers' visual attention was directed towards were:

- the centre of the logo (the blue-coloured area and the rounded shapes);
- then the red arrow;
- and finally the upper point of the blue arrow.

Afterwards those taking part in this neuroscience research were told that there was a 'C' in the logo. As a consequence we obtained the results shown in Figure 4.10.

FIGURE 4.10

After being told about the presence of the Carrefour 'C', visual attention switched to focus more on the white area of the shape. So, before being told about the 'C', the perception of the logo was more diffuse (centrifugal perspective), but afterwards visual perception made an effort to concentrate (centripetal perspective).

The external reality reaches our mind through the senses (feelings and perceptions). But when you tell someone, tell their mind, about a specific phenomenon, this information changes its perception of reality, influencing later feelings and perceptions.

Recently, Carrefour has produced different versions of its logo where the 'C' appears more clearly; see Figure 4.11.

FIGURE 4.11

This phenomenon in the perception of the Carrefour logo is part of what in psychology is called 'bistable perception'. Let's look at Figure 4.12 as another example. There are two ways of looking at this image: two faces looking at each other, or a drinking vessel.

FIGURE 4.12

In Figure 4.13 you can see a man playing a musical instrument (saxophone), or the silhouette of the head/face of a woman.

The black area conveys more of the image of a man playing a sax, while the white area brings to mind the face of a woman.

FIGURE 4.13

FIGURE 4.14

And, finally, in Figure 4.14 you can see a young woman or an old one. The face of the young woman is the nose of the old woman. The necklace or choker on the young woman is the mouth of the old woman. The ear of the young woman is the old lady's eye.

The peculiar nature of bistable perceptions is that when you are looking at one of the two possible perceptions/interpretations, you can't see the other. They are 'incompatible' when being viewed at the same time.

Summary of key learning points about brands

- The analysis of the FedEx logo brings us to a significant conclusion for marketing, advertising and media professionals: any marketing activity that is carried out involving brands must be significant in the minds of consumers.

- This may be with logos, new product ideas, advertising campaigns, packaging, promotions ... marketing activities must not go unnoticed. To be significant they have to be noticed, they have to have an impact and be relevant to the consumer. If they are too subtle they will not connect with the target audience.

- Marketing activities involving brands have to grab consumers' attention, connect with their emotions and become part of their memory.

Careful!
Watch out!

05

> *Mental power is achieved like physical power, through constant exercise.*
>
> **CHARLES FRANCIS HAANEL**

Our environment is overflowing

As we pointed out in the previous chapter, external reality bombards our five senses on a daily basis. Every second we receive huge numbers of stimuli. The world around us is full of information.

Let us think about marketing in our daily lives. If we switch on the television, we see huge numbers of ads intended to seduce us into buying the product or service they are advertising. We log on to the computer and go on to the internet, and ads invade the screen trying to grab our attention. We go to the supermarket to do the shopping, and the shelves are full of products all packaged in a way intended to hold our interest and fill that gap in our shopping trolley.

The fact is there are too many stimuli. We are saturated. In front of us are a myriad of options and we can only look at a few. Thank goodness our brain and mind are equipped with an amazing and complex piece of software: attention. Attention is like a spotlight highlighting a specific stimulus. It is like a torch lighting up the visual field. Paying attention means picking out or selecting specific information and discarding the rest. Attention is a dynamic process, in which stimuli compete to be chosen.

Imagine that you are in front of a computer with hundreds of files on the screen. Attention is like choosing one of these many files and opening it. It is an exercise involving concentrating on specific information.

Attention works in close collaboration with the five senses. It is natural to associate attention and sight (visual attention). The same occurs with the pairing of attention and hearing (auditory attention), and it applies to smell, taste and touch too. Attention helps the senses and perception in choosing information coming in from external sources.

Attention in action: in the supermarket or the disco

We have to distinguish between two types of attention: exogenous attention, which comes from the outside-in – the stimuli from the environment are dynamic and attract our attention; and endogenous attention, which works from the inside-out – our mind has a goal, an intention, a need, a desire according to which we choose specific elements from the environment.

For example, we are shopping in the hypermarket. Before we left home we made a list of all the items we must not forget. This list uses *endogenous attention*, because it will force our attention to concentrate on specific retail areas, on certain shelves and on specific products. The products will be chosen according to our needs. At the same time, there are products on the shelves that catch our attention for a variety of reasons: they are new, they have attractive packaging, they are on special offer, they have been displayed in a prime position on the gondola, etc. This phenomenon is called *endogenous perception*.

Let us now imagine that we are in a disco, or a club. There are a lot of stimuli that might grab our attention: visual (people, lighting, technical equipment, furniture); auditory (music, people singing, conversations competing with the music); tastes (drinks, an intense kiss on the mouth); olfactory (whisky, tobacco) and tactile (taking the hand of your partner, dancing close together, the glass with the drink). We may see someone dressed in a very striking fashion, or we may hear a glass being broken. These perceptive phenomena form part of what is known as *exogenous attention*. These are external stimuli that stand out from all the sensorial information washing over us. But as we go back to the bar to order a drink and try to look for our partner in the midst of the crowd on the dance floor, this is a different situation. In this instance, our mind is looking for a specific stimulus; it is looking for a body shape, a size, a hairstyle, specific clothing, a predominant colour, etc. This situation is part of the phenomenon of *endogenous perception*. Sifting through and choosing from these stimuli is carried out in line with an individual's needs and desires.

Brands, ad campaigns, slogans, logos, packaging and labels ... everything is intended to capture buyers' attention. Mature markets are saturated; offers outweigh demand; there are too many options to choose from. This is why it is important to be very efficient in our marketing activities.

Manufacturers are seeking to make an impact, to surprise and to connect with consumers. Sometimes they achieve this through originality, innovation or the relevance of the message to the target audience. When the mind is too accustomed to a stimulus it stops responding, a psychological mechanism known as 'habituation'. This is why very dynamic brands have to continue reinventing, innovating and surprising consumers in a positive way. Launching innovative products revitalizes the impact and image of the brand.

A relationship can be established between the bottom-up information path (feelings, perceptions and interpretations) and exogenous attention. In the same way, a relationship can be established between the top-down route and endogenous attention.

Differences between perception and attention

To establish the difference between perception and attention, I suggest we do a simple exercise I read about in a book by the famous Spanish psychologist, José Luis Pinillos.

First of all, don't look at your wristwatch. Pick up a piece of paper and try to draw the details of your watch. Once you have finished compare your drawing to the original. You have probably realized that there are some significant differences. How is it possible, given the number of times throughout the day that you look at your watch to find out the time? The reason is that although we look at the watch, we are only paying attention to the relevant information – what time it is. By doing this our minds conserve energy because there is no reason to pay attention to every single detail of the watch.

Psychophysiological basis for attention

Attention is a fairly complicated mental function involving various areas of the brain. In general there are three main systems taking part:

1 the arousal or alert system (reticular activating system);

2 posterior or perceptive attention – this means choosing information according to priority; it involves the right parietal lobe and its multitude of cortical and subcortical connections; and

3 anterior or supervisory attention, which takes charge of regulating the direction and object of attention. This is a fairly advanced function and relies on frontal lobe activity.

Summary of key learning points about brands

- Brands, ad campaigns, slogans, logos, packaging and labels ... everything is intended to capture buyers' attention. Mature markets are saturated; offers outweigh demand; there are too many options to choose from. This is why it is important to be very efficient in our marketing activities.

- Manufacturers seek to make an impact, to surprise and to connect with consumers. Sometimes they achieve this through originality, innovation or the relevance of the message to the target audience.

- When the mind is too accustomed to a stimulus it stops responding, a psychological mechanism known as 'habituation'. This is why very dynamic brands have to continue reinventing, innovating and surprising consumers in a positive way. Launching innovative products revitalizes the impact and image of the brand.

Do you remember?

06

> **"** *The worst derangement of the spirit is to believe things because we want them to be so.*   JACQUES BENIGNE BOSSUET

Our memory and Google

A major part of each of our individual identities is made up of our memory. Our memory records our experiences throughout our lives. Memory has a very important role in configuring the concept we call self; it provides continuity for the image of the self. Memory is like the software of knowledge and experience (learning).

We can make many comparisons and use several different metaphors to understand the function and functioning of human memory. For instance, it is like a library full of books. To find a copy, we use the title, author or subject of the book. Another analogy is a filing cabinet full of documents. If it is well organized by subject, or in alphabetical order, it will be easy to find a specific document. Much closer to the reality of our memory is the 'memory' of a computer, its hard disk.

The Google search engine is currently the closest thing we have to our brain's long-term memory. The work carried out by Google is similar to the work that the largest libraries in the ancient world used to carry out, when they collected all the knowledge of the age. Remember for example the work of the scribe, or the role played by the famous library in Alexandria. Google can be compared to the efforts France made during the Enlightenment (18th century) to compile knowledge, when Diderot, D'Alembert and Voltaire spearheaded the creation of the encyclopaedia.

We could say that Google currently fulfils the function of being humanity's collective memory. It works in a very similar way to how our own individual memories work; it is very intuitive. Intuitive brands are successful, because consumers understand them very well. This is the case with recent innovations from Apple (iPod, iPhone, iPad), the features offered by BlackBerry or Nokia mobile phones.

I have compared our memory to a library, a filing system, even a hard drive; but the problem is that these examples are merely static analogies and as such they have limitations. I prefer the example of the Google search engine. But our memory is even more lively and dynamic than any of these analogies. It is a type of organized disorder, where everything is linked by topics or by significance.

José Antonio Marina, in *El cerebro infantil: una gran oportunidad* (The infant brain: a great opportunity) says:

> Memory is not a file of photographs. It is not a warehouse where we store memories. Nor is it, as St Augustine said, a prestigious hall. There is nothing static about it. As Damasio says, what is stored in the memory are 'dispositions', 'dynamic outlines' to rebuild experiences. It is more like a cookbook of recipes than frozen dinners stored in the freezer. Remembering is reconstructing a memory.

We have many types of memory

Although the Google search engine is a good analogy for the human memory, the latter is even more complex and dynamic. We have to differentiate between the various types of memory in our brain:

- The five senses.
- Procedural memory versus declarative memory.
- Long-term memory (LTM) versus short-term memory (STM).
- Rational memory versus emotional memory.
- Conscious memory versus unconscious memory.

The five senses

We have to distinguish between visual, auditory, olfactory, taste and touch memories.

The senses of sight and hearing are predominant in human beings. Sometimes we say that someone has a good visual memory (or photographic memory): they are capable of looking closely at a document and learning its contents very quickly. There are people who have a good olfactory memory and instantly recognize a smell or a place. These sense memories were working before we were really conscious of them. For example, the sense of touch – on our skin – we were recording these experiences from the moment we were born. The way we were picked up when we were babies, the way we were cuddled, etc, have been recorded, combining information from this sense of touch and our emotions. All this before our thought processes and consciousness begin to work – we are fantastic beings.

Some authors (such as Didier Anzieu) have developed the ideas of a 'skin self', which is a very primitive level of memory that has been configured in the mind, taking account of only the corporeal aspect and the information we receive through the sense of touch.

Procedural memory versus declarative memory

Procedural memory comes into play when we use our motor skills: it carries them out habitually and automatically. When it comes to learning, it is the frontal and temporal lobes that spring into action, but when what we have learnt becomes automatic it tends to be delegated to the level 1 brain structures: the cerebellum and other subcortical areas.

Declarative memory is made up of two modules: semantic memory containing the information learnt from the world that surrounds us, ie what we know – this knowledge tends to be fairly well organized by categories; and episodic or autobiographical memory, which records our experiences according to time-space parameters (they are structured in relation to the time and place of the event).

Long-term memory (LTM) versus short-term memory (STM)

LTM records information in a way that retains it over time. STM, now better known as working memory or active memory, only works for a short time, a few seconds.

For example, someone may give me a phone number that I am going to use immediately and I do not need to memorize it. This phone number, for example the customer services number for my credit card, will only stay in my mind for a very short time. If I want to move it to my LTM I have to use learning software to save it and to be able to recall it in the future. Repetition, learning and memory work closely together to build very effective neuronal circuits so, unlike the credit card phone number, the phone numbers we use most often come most readily to mind.

Rational memory versus emotional memory

There is one facet of the memory relating to thoughts/ideas/contents (rational level) and another that records the valence of events (emotional level), which might be positive, negative or neutral. We have already seen that emotions appear to evolve before thoughts. This implies that there are aspects of our emotional life, of which we are unaware, that are recorded in our brain.

Conscious memory versus unconscious memory

We are not conscious of all the information that is recorded in our memory. The unconscious part can greatly influence our life, our decisions and our behaviour. As we will see later, in the chapter on happiness, the more conscious we are of how our mind functions, the more likely we are to be happy, because we can better regulate and coordinate our thoughts, communications, actions, expectations, desires, etc.

We have one type of memory relating to knowledge (called semantic memory), another relating to emotions and yet another that involves actions.

Memory and senses

Generally we are more conscious of our visual and auditory memories than our olfactory, taste or touch memories. However, there is great variation between individuals. From the time we are born (including during the gestation period in the mother's womb) our senses begin to record our experiences.

But consciousness is not there when we are born; it appears progressively. How old were you when you had your first memory? Although it varies a lot between people, our first childhood memories tend to appear at three, four or five years of age. This means that some of the experiences that we had during early infancy, in the first few years of life, were recorded but not in a conscious fashion.

For example, the sense of touch perceives how we are held when we were small, and whether those hands and arms that were in direct contact with our skin were affectionate or not. These feelings remain recorded even though we are not aware of them, and so we do not have access to this material. Regular patterns of behaviour, such as picking up a small child, giving it a bottle, bathing it, dressing it, etc can have a determining influence on the child's future confidence and self-esteem when he or she is an adult.

Last week I was in a shopping centre and saw a mother playing with her daughter. The little girl was about three years old, and she was climbing onto a bench and throwing herself into her mother's arms. She was very excited and repeated the game over and over again. Every time the little girl jumped, her mother caught her. This childlike game, so innocent and natural, was configuring this little girl's basic trust.

During the first two years of life, before the child can understand our verbal language, a host of expectations, intentions, desires, and meanings are being conveyed through non-verbal language, by touch, by emotions and so on. We are so used to communicating through language that we are not aware of the importance of non-verbal communication: sight (looking), physical contact (touch), the body (stance), the face (gestures), etc.

Oddly enough, every year at school pupils study 'language'. It refers to verbal language – they are not taught about non-verbal language; they are not told about communicating through facial gestures and body language, which can be really important at times in our life. Non-verbal communication is key to our relationships with others, and they can give us important clues to the 'true' emotions or intentions of a person.

Working memory

Traditional psychology distinguishes between short-term memory (STM) and long-term memory (LTM). The former is able to retain information for only a few seconds. Once this brief time has passed, it is necessary to learn/record it on LTM if the information is not to be lost.

The latest discoveries in neuroscience have identified the hippocampus as the LTM organizer. The word 'hippocampus' comes from Greek and means 'seahorse', because of its shape. While it is believed that the hippocampus is directly related to information storage, it does not mean that this small part of the brain 'dispenses' or 'stores' memory. It seems that the hippocampus works like a librarian, but there are information files throughout the brain's cortex. Neurones themselves are even thought to be involved in this activity. Memory is a complex function that needs brain activity as a whole.

Joaquín Fuster, a world authority in the field of neurology, says about memory:

> Memory is a functional property, among others, of each and all of the areas of the cerebral cortex, and thus all cortical systems. Furthermore, as the cortex engages in representing and acting on the world, memory in one form or another is an integral part of all operations. Thus, as one of the cognitive functions of the cerebral cortex, memory is global and nonlocalizable.

Javier Tirapu, in his book *¿Para qué sirve el cerebro? manual para principiantes* (What is the brain for? A manual for beginners), says, 'Currently, memory processes are conceived as a function of the brain acting as a whole.'

Ideas about STM have undergone some changes and it is currently referred to as 'working memory'. Working memory is a complex concept referring to a system that holds and handles information on a temporary basis. Working memory works closely with attention and LTM and involves frontal lobe activity.

Working memory is like having lots of files open on your computer and working on several of them at the same time. When this is the case, we cannot pay real attention to such a volume and variety of information.

Memory constructs and reconstructs

Human memory is fascinating. It is very lively and dynamic; it is not just a computer recovering information. Because our memory records events, it is capable of recovering them and also reconstructing them. Some memories are objective, others are more subjective. Sometimes memory can complete or gloss over recollections. The relationship between memory and the emotional system influences the quality and significance of memories.

It is curious to see how sometimes, when several people have experienced and lived through the same event, they remember it differently. Our personality and emotional systems interact with our memory and add that personal touch to the contents of what we remember:

> Rather than recovering faithful copies of these experiences, we recreate and reconstruct them, in the process adding feelings, beliefs, even knowledge gained after the experience, to the reconstruction. We influence our reminiscences, stored as sepia-coloured photos in our memory, adding colour from our emotions and information acquired after the event.
>
> (Javier Tirapu, ¿*Para qué sirve el cerebro? manual para principiantes*)

Learning and memory are very closely related. When we learn something new, or establish a relationship between different events in our mind, the wiring (neural circuits) in our brain changes. The new learning experiences are recorded on our memory.

As with the rest of the brain, the memory function has evolved over time, becoming more complex, assuming new functions and offering more facilities. Working memory is one of the latest developments.

Mistakes in using names

Often, even if we know a person really well, we forget to use their correct name. In my case, this is getting more common, and I am also quite absent-minded.

I may call a colleague Nieves instead of Reyes, or a client Reyes when her name is Nieves. If we focus closely on these mistakes, we see that it involves names that have a phonetic or semantic similarity. In the case of these two names (Nieves and Reyes) there is some phonetic similarity. They are two disyllabic words, with a similar pronunciation. This means that they are stored very close together in the same memory 'box', which is why sometimes when we go to pick one, we pick the other. In addition, they are both feminine names (in Spanish) that have other similarities, for example neither of them is very common in Spain nowadays.

This can also happen with the male names such as Adolfo and Alfredo; trisyllabic names beginning with the letter 'A' and ending in the letter 'o' (these are not common male names either). So, we are confronted with the same phenomenon: you go to pick one and come up with the other by mistake. My colleague Adolfo often gets called Alfredo or Alfonso. This is why we might say we have been for a drink in a bar called 'Alfredo's', when in actual fact we have been to 'Arturo's'.

However, this issue can be even more difficult. Very often when I want to call one of my children, for example, David, I say Patricia, and vice versa. These two names are totally different in terms of phonetics, and one is masculine, the other is feminine. But we have to take into account the fact that the memory has catalogued them as children of Elena and Pepe. They are stored this way in that file. If I try to access one, I might pick the other one by mistake.

The way memory functions is impressive, and it has an incredible capacity for cataloguing information. It uses multiple cataloguing and classification criteria for filing away all the objects, ideas and experiences from the world that surrounds us. It transforms the external reality into an internal 'warehouse' that tries to be as objective as it can, but an individual's personality, experiences and emotions have an influence on this filing task.

For this reason, external reality is 'objective' and our internal world is 'subjective'. The ancient Greeks used to say that we should be very careful with our feelings because they can 'deceive' us.

A research study on remembering advertising slogans

In September 2009 we carried out a market research study to find out which advertising campaign slogans in the different media had captured consumers' attention and remained recorded in their memory. The research was set up as follows:

- The study population consisted of members of the general public aged between 18 and 75.
- Area: Spain (Peninsula, Balearic Islands and Canary Islands).
- Technique: Computer Assisted Telephone Interviewing system (CATI).
- Sample: 1,000 interviews from the reference population.
- Sample design: representative of a national level by region and 'habitat', with quotas for sex, age and social class.
- Questionnaire: two completely spontaneous questions in Week 38 of 2009.
- Fieldwork: all the interviews were carried out by a full-time team and an expert in telephone interviews from Millward Brown. Specifically, 38 interviewers and three supervisors worked on this research.

The two questions asked were: 'Think of advertising, whether on television, press, radio, or any other means of communication. Can you tell me which slogans come to mind? Any other?' and, 'Can you tell me what brand it is for?'

This mental exercise is not easy. We try to put ourselves in this situation: an unknown person calls you on the phone and asks you, just like that, for ad slogans. It is like a surprise test, without the opportunity to study for it.

The results of the study highlighted the fact that 77 per cent of those interviewed were unable to recall any slogans, while 23 per cent searched their memory and managed to come up with something. Among the participants who attempted an answer (230 people), they found it easier to remember details of an ad, talking about the brand or the benefits of the product or service, than reproducing the slogan. I will stress again, the specificity of the questions means that answering was not easy.

These were the responses from the 230 individuals who remembered a slogan:

- 8 per cent remembered the slogans *'La chispa de la vida'* (The spark of life) (Coca-Cola) and *'Donde caben dos caben tres'* (Where you can fit two, you can fit three) (Ikea).
- 7 per cent remembered *'Ya lo sabía'* (I knew it!) (ING).
- 6 per cent remembered *'¿Te gusta conducir?'* (Do you like driving?) (BMW).
- 3 per cent remembered *'Piensa en verde'* (Think green) (Heineken) and *'Si bebes no conduzcas'* (If you drink, don't drive) (Dirección General de Tráfico).
- 2 per cent remembered *'Donde va triunfa'* (Where it goes, it succeeds) (San Miguel beer), 'Just do it' (Nike), *'La calidad no es cara'* (Quality isn't expensive) (Lidl) and *'Porque tú lo vales'* (Because you're worth it) (L'Oreal).

The first slogan, the one that was remembered the most (by 8 per cent of the population), is a claim that the Coca-Cola brand has been using for many years. It is a very successful phrase that captures consumers' attention and is firmly embedded in their minds. It is a positive, optimistic message that invites you to enjoy life and to live it to the full. *'La chispa de la vida'* (The spark of life) invites you into a world of happiness. It is a way of entering into the mind of consumers, using positive messages that connect directly with their needs and desires, and with their emotions.

The second advertising phrase, *'Donde caben dos caben tres'* (Where you can fit two, you can fit three) is from IKEA. Unlike Coca-Cola's slogan, this is a fairly recent claim. However, the company is using a colloquial phrase heard in many Spanish homes when more people than expected turn up to lunch, dinner or to stay overnight; there is always room for one more. It is a positive message, about opening up to others, cohabitation, solidarity and collective enjoyment. Also, in this instance it is accompanied by a catchy jingle. It is a way of creating a space in consumers' minds; using a familiar saying and combining it with striking and engaging music.

The same can be said of the third most remembered advertising phrase, *'Ya lo sabía'* (I knew it!) from ING. Once again it involves a colloquialism and once again it combines it with catchy music. The result is the same: it captures the consumers' attention and they save it on the hard disk in their mind. The expression, 'I knew it!' is an excellent reflection of everyone's wish to be able to correctly predict the future and to be more intelligent than everyone else.

So, when building a slogan or choosing a good claim for a brand, we have to consider several aspects. On the formal level (external aspects of the phrase and the phonetic dimension): is it a short, striking and catchy phrase;

does it have a hook? It has to be like a dart, forcefully striking the target audience's mind – will it be easy to remember or reproduce? On the semantic level (internal aspects of the message; content, meaning): does it invoke key desires and needs in the consumer? It has to be interesting and relevant so that people choose it from among all the advertising stimuli they receive and keep it in their memory.

Obviously, expenditure on advertising is key, because the campaigns most frequently seen and heard on television, the internet, radio, etc have the highest probability of being remembered. However, this is not just an issue of quantity; it is, above all, a question of connecting with the consumer (engagement). It means having an impact, and capturing and influencing the consumer.

Designing questionnaires or drawing up guidelines

Drafting a questionnaire is one of the most important activities a quantitative researcher carries out. For a qualitative technician, preparing guidelines for a group meeting or an in-depth interview is equally important.

Why? Because the responses we receive depend on the questions we ask. The type of information we obtain depends on the questions we ask. Good questions lead to good responses. Sometimes we do not receive the most relevant or appropriate information because we have not asked a specific question or because we have not framed it in the most suitable way.

We have to think very carefully about what will be the key to opening the consumer's mind; in other words, what will be the most appropriate question to bring us the information we are looking for. We must distinguish between the various types of questions:

1 Open ('What is happiness for you?') versus closed ('What brand of shower gel do you use?')

2 The dichotomous question (asking for a 'Yes' or a 'No') 'Do you usually have orange juice for breakfast?'

3 The direct question ('What is your driving style?') versus the indirect question where we allow a pause for the mind of the interviewee to be able to project ('How do people tend to drive these days?')

4 The rational question ('What are the features of the Nespresso brand?') versus the emotional question ('How do you feel when you are drinking Nespresso coffee?'; 'When I talk about the Nespresso brand, what images come into your mind?' or 'What feelings come to mind?')

Each one of these questions activates the consumer's memory in a different way and takes him or her down specific neural pathways to give access to a particular type of information. This is often why, at qualitative group meetings, the moderator tries different types of questions or different formulations to ensure that he or she has accessed all the relevant information on the topic being discussed.

Summary of key learning points about brands

When creating an advertising slogan or choosing a good claim for the brand, two important aspects must be taken into account: it should be a short, impressive and sonorous (catchy) phrase – this way it will be easy to remember and reproduce (Nike: 'Just do it'); and it should be relevant to consumers, ie it connects with their needs, emotions, desires and expectations (Nokia: 'Connecting people').

Wonderful!

07

> *Let's not forget that the little emotions are the great captains of our lives and we obey them without realizing it.*
>
> VINCENT VAN GOGH

The origins of the word 'emotion'

If we consult Wikipedia, we will find that the word 'emotion' has its roots in the Latin word *'emotio-onis'*, referring to an impulse leading to an action. It also gives us a good definition of emotions, presenting them as psychological phenomena representing ways of adapting to certain environmental situations or one's particular state. Emotions are a very interesting phenomenon, because they are midway between biology (the body), psychology (the mind) and sociology (our relationships with others).

There are two books by the famous neuroscientist, Antonio Damasio: *Looking for Spinoza: Joy, sorrow and the feeling brain,* and *Descartes' Error: Emotion, reason and the human brain.* Why would Damasio choose these two rationalist philosophers for the titles of his books? Because, despite both having lived fairly close to each other, in more or less the same era, they put forward very different ways of seeing the world. Descartes was born in La Haye en Touraine in 1596 and died in 1650. Spinoza was born in Amsterdam in 1632 and died in 1677.

For Descartes the body (the corporeal substance, *res extensa*) is of a completely different nature to the soul (the mental substance, *res cogitans*). They involve two very different levels, practically independent of each other. They are only joined through the coordination of the pineal gland. For Spinoza, there is a continuum between the body, the mind and the world. His theory includes the concept of energy. Damasio is of the opinion that Descartes was wrong, and that Spinoza, on the other hand, offered many clues in establishing a continuum between physiology, psychology and the world that surrounds us. Descartes set out a dualist philosophy, separating the body from the mind. Spinoza developed a pantheistic focus, where there is close integration and continuity between the ideas of body, mind and world (including God).

The emotions are a perfect example of how everything in our body works as an interrelated whole. When we experience an emotion, our body and our state of mind react at the same time, in a synchronized fashion. Emotions flood our whole being and make us react as a whole. Emotions colour our lives. In general terms, our daily experiences can be:

- Positive: involving agreeable and positive situations we would like to repeat.
- Negative: the complete opposite; unpleasant situations we would like to avoid.
- Neutral: situations of a middling nature; they leave us fairly indifferent; we neither want to repeat nor avoid them.

We tend to repeat behaviours that make us feel good, for which we feel rewarded or psychologically stronger. We tend to avoid behaviours that make us feel bad, for which we feel psychologically 'punished'. Let's think of a plant. Its behaviour, which is pretty basic, consists of seeking water and light, and avoiding drought and darkness. We, obviously, are more complex than vegetation, but in a very similar way we also look for pleasure, well-being, recognition and affection. We veer away from displeasure, illness, indifference and a lack of recognition and psychological mistreatment.

There are many classifications of basic emotions. Some talk of four, others of five, six or even eight. The idea of basic emotions refers to an experience that is very closely linked to the body and that is present in all humans, at all times and in all cultures. Here I have used one of these many classifications; this one includes six basic emotions:

1 *Happiness:* a positive emotion, directly related to everything that makes us feel good on all levels.
2 *Sadness:* the opposite emotion to happiness (and therefore has negative valence).
3 *Fear:* a very important emotion because it acts to protect the individual and the species. Although it has a negative valence, it fulfils the survival function. It sounds a warning and alerts the person to mortal danger.
4 *Surprise:* the emotional reaction to an unanticipated or new situation. It may have a positive or negative valence, depending on the content of the surprise.
5 *Anger:* a negative reaction of a hostile or aggressive nature, as a consequence of something in the individual's environment having an impact on them and leaving them in a situation of impotence, weakness, dependence, injustice, etc.
6 *Disgust or aversion:* a negative emotional reaction, both physical and psychological, when confronted with unpleasant or repugnant objects or situations.

These basic emotions become more complex as the individual matures, giving rise to more sophisticated psychological experiences, such as state of mind or feelings. Emotions are more related to the body. State of mind and feelings, although also linked to the body, are more related to the mind (psychological dimension).

What is our relationship with our emotions?

Our emotions follow us throughout our lives, from the moment we are born, even during gestation. Strangely enough, we rarely receive training or coaching on how to manage emotions. It is a situation very similar to creativity. Both the emotions and a sense of creativity are very important in life, but schools, colleges and universities are more focused on acquiring knowledge.

Our culture has probably been too focused on controlling our emotions. Emotions are considered to be a negative reaction by the body, and need to be monitored closely. On many occasions this has led to emotions being repressed. Both repression and denial of emotions are prejudicial to a person's health. Emotions are energy. If that energy (positive or negative) is not freed, the person cannot establish a good relationship with the environment that surrounds them. The ideal is to live in emotional homeostasis (balance) with everyone else.

The concept of homeostasis comes from biology and refers to a balanced exchange with the surrounding media. For example, any cell in our body has to have a good interchange function; taking up the substances that allow it to feed and carry out its life function, and depositing its waste substances. The term 'homeostasis' comes from the Greek 'homos' (similar) and 'estasis' (stability). It refers to a system's capacity to maintain a stable equilibrium. In terms of emotions, we have to listen to our emotional system and we have to react according to the stimuli that reach us from others. If they treat us well and show concern for our well-being, we have to show them our satisfaction and gratitude. If, on the other hand, they treat us badly, we have to show our dissatisfaction and act in a way so that in future they avoid this type of behaviour.

If a person, A, abuses, mistreats or causes negative emotions in another person, B, the logical thing would be for B to protest and show his or her discomfort to A. But human beings are not completely logical or rational. Sometimes, common sense is the least common of all the senses. And it might be that B tells a third person (C) about his or her unhappy situation, but the fact that C knows about the situation will not change A's behaviour. It is advisable to always be aware of the importance of showing our emotions to the appropriate person in a mature and effective way.

Managing emotions has a direct impact on a person's happiness. We may meet people who abuse these emotions and use them to manipulate others instead of using them as an instrument for communication. This is an overreaction:

> Anyone can become angry – that is easy, but to be angry with the right person at the right time, and for the right purpose and in the right way – that is not within everyone's power and that is not easy. (Aristotle)

Since we receive almost no education about our emotions, many people find it difficult to relate to their emotions and handle them appropriately and effectively in interactions with others. Emotions ought to come with a manual, and we should be taught about them at school while we are still young.

We have to establish an internal dialogue with our emotions in order to negotiate and deal with them. We should not eliminate them from our lives. Emotions are the psychophysiological solutions belonging to our species, so that we can better adapt to the environment around us.

If the frontal lobe, the conscious and rational part of a person's brain, does not listen to the limbic system (emotional brain) it can create multiple problems. This means that if our emotional needs are not tended from above, from the 'control tower', from the rational brain, what will happen? They can go downwards rapidly, towards the body. We have already said that emotions are halfway between biology and psychology. If the psychological application or 'authority' does not take notice, they turn to biology. They look for an outlet through the body. This is the world of psychosomatic reality. They begin to work on some part or organ of the body (headaches, nausea, the heart, the stomach, the skin, etc).

It is their way of protesting that we have not listened to them and involves creating either biological or physiological symptoms, dysfunctions or diseases. If they do not find an upward outlet (the mind), they move downwards (the body) and act as if they were 'on strike'. There is a saying in Spain that if something cannot leave through the door, it will go out the window, meaning that if emotions are unable to surface normally, they will find another outlet. Emotions are like water, always finding a way out. Emotions are energy, they don't disappear magically. Remember what the laws of physics teach us: energy is neither created nor destroyed, it can only be transformed.

One of the greatest influences on people in terms of success in their career, with their partner, family, friends, their relationship with their boss, with colleagues, clients, suppliers, etc is the way emotions are handled. People who know how to listen to their emotions, how to incorporate them into their lives and convey them appropriately to others are happier, because they are more genuine, more true to themselves.

When we refuse to have anything to do with our emotions (denial, repression), we need to spend a great deal of energy in stopping them reaching our conscious level. However, if we are prepared to have a dialogue with them, listen to them, negotiate with them and integrate them into our lives, at that precise moment we will free up all that extra energy and we can use it to carry out other activities. Our body works like a battery: if we use it properly it can generate more energy.

It is very useful to learn about geography, history, biology, physics, chemistry, etc. But believe me, in life, being able to manage our emotions is a better predictor of our personal and professional success than knowing the name of the tallest mountain in Germany or the world's biggest ocean.

Where are emotions born and where do they live?

Intuitively we relate thought to the head and the brain, and emotions to the heart. What is this? It is obvious that thoughts come from the head, but it is not true that emotions are born in the heart.

The emotions are found in an area close to the centre of the brain, known as the limbic system. It is also known as the 'emotional brain' because it is responsible for our emotions. This area of the brain is connected to the autonomic nervous system (ANS), responsible for conveying emotion to the body, for example, an increased heartbeat. This is one of the reasons why emotions are thought of as directly related to the heart.

Emotions are born in the limbic system, they are 'felt' in the prefrontal cortex and become manifest in the body. Figure 7.1 shows the position of the limbic system in the brain. Within the limbic system the amygdala has a protagonist role. It gets its name from the Greek for its almond-like

FIGURE 7.1

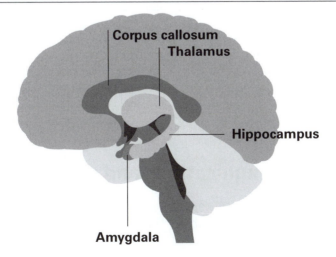

shape. The amygdala is a sensor, a very sensitive alarm that warns the body, the individual, of any external danger.

Information coming from the outside can follow two routes to reach the brain and deliver its message. One is the 'normal' route, the cortical pathway, also known as the conscious route. Feelings become perceptions and then they are analysed by the cerebral cortex. Although everything is carried out very quickly, this route is much slower than the 'urgent' route, the subcortical pathway, also known as the unconscious or automatic route. Feelings become perceptions, they quickly reach the amygdala, which sounds the alarm immediately in the cerebral cortex. The amygdala's mission is to warn us of danger or threatening situations.

Mirror neurones

Between 1980 and 1990, in Parma (Italy) Giacomo Rizzolatti, another important figure in the field of neuroscience, discovered mirror neurones, also known as the 'empathy neurones'.

Rizzolatti was working in the laboratory researching monkeys. One of the members of the research team decided to have something to eat. At that precise moment the technological equipment in the brain of the monkey they were monitoring began to register brain activity. It produced a mental impression of the behaviour of eating. The neurones that register this type of brain activity are known as 'mirror neurones'. A major part of human learning is down to these neurones. We learn by imitating others, whether these are the things we like to do or the things we have to avoid.

When we are in the cinema we identify with the people in the film, and experience in our brain the same reactions as they are living. The only difference is that we, the observers, do not move. Mirror neurones put us in someone else's place. The publicist's goal is to achieve that effect when we are watching an advertisement: that we live the situations, the product or service like the characters in the ad, that we feel the same sensations and that in the end we buy that brand.

The same happens when we are in a restaurant and see that one of the other diners close to our table is really enjoying the dish he or she is eating. Mirror neurones help us put ourselves in their place and, so, ask the waiter for the same dish. Mirror neurones put us in connection with the emotions and thoughts of other people. They help us learn without having to have lived or experienced a specific situation.

Brands, communications and emotions

Between 2001 and 2003 Millward Brown carried out an analysis of 6,065 brands, using the BrandZ database. As you can see from the graph in Figure 7.2, emotionally attractive brands are stronger brands.

FIGURE 7.2 Emotionally attractive brands are stronger brands

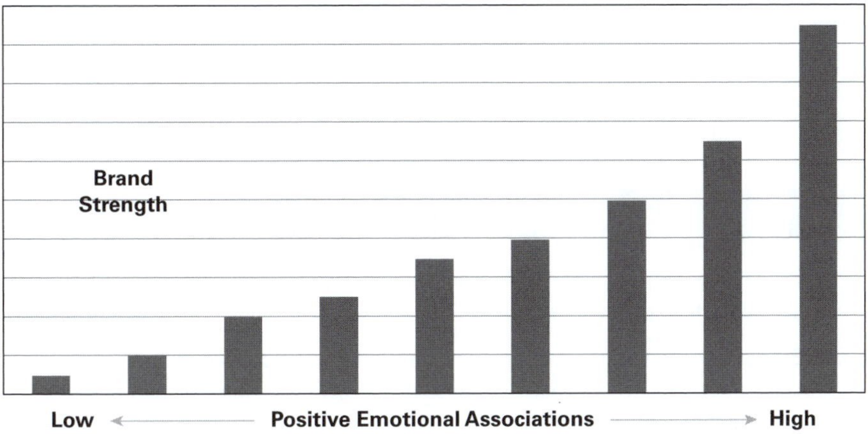

Brand
Strength

Low ← — Positive Emotional Associations — → High

SOURCE: BrandZ database, 6,065 brands 2001–2003

Brands and their corresponding communications connect with consumers' positive emotions, because they know that is the best way to make an impact on them and enter into their minds. The emotional system is closely related to attention, memory and perception. The consumer's attention can be captured through emotions, and this becomes part of his or her memory.

A brand's objective is to generate a good experience for consumers through its various actions and communications. This means generating what is known as a 'positive brand experience'. This involves stimulating positive feelings and emotions so that the consumer wants to repeat this situation through brand loyalty. It is essential to understand consumers' attitudes and beliefs to be able to orientate brand strategy and advertising campaigns in the right direction. When we talk of beliefs, we do not mean religious beliefs, but the values that guide buyer behaviour and consumption of products and services.

Attitudes and beliefs are very important because they cement cognitive (thought) and emotional-type structures. They are recorded in consumers' minds and determine much of their buying behaviour. Communications should be focused on taking advantage of specific beliefs if these are favourable for our brand's objectives, or to deactivate them if the wind is not blowing in our favour. Attitudes and beliefs are the outcome of knowledge, experience and emotion. Until we experience something for ourselves it remains hearsay, a suggestion or a claim and we are not willing to take conscious ownership of the idea.

Consumer insight is a type of attitude or belief that lives inside the mind of consumers in relation to a brand, product or service. As market researchers, we have to determine the current 'consumer insight' to be able to design an appropriate marketing strategy. 'Sight' means vision or view, and 'in' means within or inside. Consumer insight is the view a consumer has about a brand; it is built on certain cognitive and emotional elements, it includes conscious and unconscious aspects and it determines the consumer's attitude and behaviour towards the brand itself.

Summary of key learning points about brands

- Brands that are most intensely associated with positive emotions are the strongest in the market.

- Brands and their corresponding communications try to connect with consumers' positive emotions, because they know that is the best way to make an impact on them and enter into their minds.

- The emotional system is closely related to attention, memory and perception. The consumer's attention can be captured through emotions, and this then becomes part of his or her memory.

- A brand's objective is to generate a good experience for consumers, through its various actions and communications. This means achieving 'a positive brand experience'. This involves stimulating positive feelings and emotions, so that the consumer wants to repeat this situation through brand loyalty.

- It is essential to understand consumers' attitudes and beliefs in order to be able to orientate brand strategy and advertising campaigns in the right direction. When we talk of beliefs, we mean the values that guide buyer behaviour and consumption of products and services.

- Attitudes and beliefs are very important because they cement cognitive (thought) and emotional-type structures. They are recorded in consumers' minds and determine much of their buying behaviour. Communications should be focused on taking advantage of specific beliefs, if these are favourable for our brand's objectives, or to deactivate them if the wind is not blowing in our favour.

- Attitudes and beliefs are the product of knowledge, experience and emotion.

- Consumer insight is a type of attitude or belief that lives inside the mind of consumers in relation to a brand, product or service. As market researchers we have to determine the current 'consumer insight', to be able to design an appropriate marketing strategy.

- Consumer insight is the view a consumer has about a brand; it is built on certain cognitive and emotional elements, it includes conscious and unconscious aspects and it determines the consumer's attitude and behaviour towards the brand itself.

How clever!

08

Intelligence is not only knowledge, but also the ability to apply that knowledge into practice. **ARISTOTLE**

The classical approach to intelligence

Until the latter part of the 20th century the concept of intelligence was closely linked to the amount of knowledge a person had acquired. This meant that the focus was mainly on the quantitative dimension: intelligence was seen as a quantity of knowledge. Therefore, pupils who obtained the best marks in exams and academic tests in schools, colleges and universities were considered to be more intelligent.

In this context, the concept of intelligence is highly conditioned by the ability to memorize information. Those pupils with good memories were more likely to be considered intelligent. From this perspective, intelligence is almost directionally proportional to a person's level of culture. Those people with a higher sociocultural level were considered more intelligent than those with a low sociocultural level.

Numerous intelligence tests were developed to calculate a person's intellectual quotient (IQ). Later it was discovered that what most of these intelligence tests mainly measured was, once again, the person's sociocultural level from the perspective of a developed country in western society. The concept of intelligence that triumphed for the greater part of the 20th century was limited, and directly related to acquired cultural knowledge. An individual was seen as cultured, not cultured, or cultured to a degree.

This focus on intelligence may be useful when it involves assessing someone who wants to become a teacher or who wants to compete in a television game show where the participants' amount of knowledge is put to the test. In both cases having more knowledge considerably increases their chances of success.

Evidence began to show that the pupils who had obtained the best grades at school and university were not necessarily those who achieved most personal and professional success in adulthood. This is because there was another type of variable at play, one that went beyond the amount of knowledge acquired and influenced a person's performance in the future. In this respect, emotional variables and adapting to environmental changes are determining factors. For example, those people who chose their profession because it was precisely the one they wanted were much happier and had achieved greater professional and personal success in their lives. In this instance it is obvious that enjoying one's professional role and being passionate about the work one does has a decisive effect. People who have a real vocation for what they do convey this attitude to other people and have a positive impact on them.

Those teachers who teach their subject with enthusiasm and passion can have a greater influence on the future professional choice of their pupils than those who don't show such emotions when they are teaching their subject, or in the professional career they are following. Enthusiasm and passion are very contagious.

A new concept of intelligence

In 1995, Daniel Goleman's book, *Emotional Intelligence*, was published. What this author describes involved a real revolution in conceptualizing intelligence.

Daniel Goleman is an American psychologist and former professor of psychology at Harvard University, editor of the journal *Psychology Today* and editor of the brain and behavioural sciences section of the *New York Times*. He became famous through his book *Emotional Intelligence*, which he followed with *Social Intelligence*.

Goleman's book significantly broadened people's concept of intelligence. They began to relate it to emotional issues. This view of intelligence extended to people's capacity to adapt to ever-changing environments. Intelligence came to be related to flexibility, to having varied and diverse repertoires of responses to face different situations.

The concept of personal intelligence or success is no longer simply a matter of the cleverest boy or girl in the class. The most intelligent is no longer the one who gets the best marks in exams. Now, the cleverest is the one with the greatest capacity for survival in different situations (ecosystems) obtaining the highest level of well-being (pleasure), both for the individual and for others. The purely rational perspective of intelligence is thus complementary to the emotional dimension. Attention is no longer excessively focused on rational intelligence, on the acquisition and demonstration of knowledge.

The mission of the brain, the mind, intelligence, is to try to ensure, as far as possible, the person's survival and well-being. Goleman says in his book:

> My concern is with a key set of these 'other characteristics', emotional
> intelligence: abilities such as being able to motivate oneself and persist in the

face of frustrations; to control impulse and delay gratification; to regulate one's moods and keep distress from swamping the ability to think; to empathize and to hope.

Wikipedia has the following definition of emotional intelligence: 'the ability, capacity, skill; or a self-perceived ability to identify, assess, and control the emotions of oneself, of others, and of groups'. However, as we have already seen with memory, there are different types of intelligence. The rational and emotional variants are two examples, but they are not the only ones. Intelligence is a very complex mental function that can be approached from different angles. There are other expressions of intelligence such as verbal intelligence, numeric intelligence and spatial intelligence.

Reason, reasoning, thought, the ability to think, in other words rational intelligence, is found in the frontal lobe. Emotions, as we saw earlier, are born in the limbic system (or emotional brain) and are felt in the prefrontal lobe. Therefore, it is important that these areas of the brain relate to each other correctly and collaborate well. This communication, or dialogue, between the prefrontal lobe and the limbic brain is crucial for making good decisions in life (personal and professional). It is the famous binomial 'reason-emotion'.

Later we will analyse the decision-making process, but for the moment we want to highlight the fact that to reach intelligent conclusions, the ideal is to combine all our mental resources at our disposal: reason plus emotion. The input reaching us from the emotional module (limbic system, amygdala) can be a deciding factor in making intelligent decisions. There has to be good coordination between the frontal lobe and the limbic system. Each has to respect and take into account the other. A good two-way pathway is required so that communication flows properly between these two areas of the brain.

Understanding our own emotions (through introspection and feedback from others) and others' emotions (through empathy and communication) is of enormous help in social relationships and makes them more satisfactory. Also, for marketers, understanding customers' emotions is often helpful in designing brand strategy and related communications. It allows us to better identify a way of connecting with consumers, making our brand stand out from the many brands, products, services and messages. It helps us create the relevant message to achieve a positive impact in the consumer's mind.

Intelligence, like all higher order mental functions, is a very complex system. It is related to several functions and abilities, including:

- attention;
- ability to learn;
- working memory and long-term memory (LTM);
- emotions, etc.

As mentioned above, the concept of intelligence has been extended. Today, being intelligent is:

- Carrying out a good analysis of the situation we find ourselves in.

- Thoroughly understanding the options of our specific situation, ie being realistic.

- Using common sense, which, as I said before, isn't all that common. It involves choosing the best solution possible. In his book, *¿Para qué sirve el cerebro? manual para principiantes* (What is the brain for? A manual for beginners), Javier Tirapu explains that: 'There is a phrase attributed to Thomas Hart, which I think is the key to life and it says, "we must have the capacity to change what we can change, the serenity to accept what we cannot change and the intelligence to distinguish between the two".'

- Confronting the different situations life throws at us, facing the problems that lie in wait and resolving them.

- Knowing how to ask, and how to ask ourselves, good questions rather than giving, or giving ourselves, the right answers to questions that are not essential. Correctly identifying relevant issues and researching the main variables that surround the key to the problem.

- Behaving in an intelligent manner, which is not at all easy. It is not just about being clever in terms of knowledge, but about using it to act in an intelligent way. It is not about talking or thinking properly, but about using executive memory and showing decision-making capabilities.

- Resolving life's practical problems, real problems rather than theoretical or imaginary ones.

- Knowing how to 'read' situations, anticipating problems and correctly predicting what is to come (the future). The frontal lobe is the area of the brain that differentiates us most from other living beings and is directly linked to foresight and planning the future.

In his book, Javier Tirapu defines intelligence as 'the encounter between the external world offering up situations that I have to resolve and my internal world that imagines solutions and outcomes to these possible solutions. Both worlds meet in the prefrontal cortex.' Elkhonon Goldberg is a famous neurologist born in Riga, Latvia, in 1946. He has focused his studies on the frontal lobes. I have included a paragraph of his on the role the frontal lobes play in the human mind:

> The executive functions of the brain are linked to intentionality, purposefulness, and complex decision making. They are located in the frontal lobes, they reach significant development only in man; arguably, they make us human. All human evolution has been classed as 'the golden age of the frontal lobes'. My mentor, Alexander Luria, called the frontal lobes 'the organ of civilization'.

I would like to highlight two of Goldberg's books: *The Executive Brain: Frontal lobes and the civilized mind* (2001) and *The New Executive Brain: Frontal lobes in a complex world* (2009), both published by Oxford University Press, New York. Another author, Eduardo Punset, in *Viaje al poder de la mente* (Journey through the power of the mind) expounds two very interesting ideas to help us better understand the new views on intelligence. First, change is a habitual state of nature. Our mind always has to be prepared to confront a changing environment. However, human beings tend towards stability and putting down roots. You have to be very careful with stagnation when you stop moving. Life is a journey, a pathway. Stopping for a rest or preparing for a new stage is one thing, but remaining permanently static is another. To stay put is to bring on atrophy. We have to bank on change, evolution and growth, whether physical, psychological or social.

Secondly, when we are little we complain about how hard it is to learn because it requires a lot of effort and discipline. It is a stage in our lives when there are many things we do not understand fully and we find it difficult to assimilate them. When we are older we find ourselves in the reverse situation: now it is difficult to unlearn things. The basic learning period of our lives serves as a guide to how we relate to other people and the world around us, but at the same time it prevents us from seeing new ways of interacting with our environment. It is important to learn, and it is also important to unlearn.

We must never lose the desire to learn new things and to continually review what we have learnt, to be able to reach a better understanding of the world and the people around us. We must carry out regular cognitive and emotional restructuring of the reality in which we live. In other words, we need to 'reset' our hard drive every so often.

The world around us is very complex. It is very difficult to explain it in a single model that we can use as a guide in our journey through life. For this reason, it is advisable to regularly review our model in light of the new experiences we have lived. In this way, the model will be increasingly comprehensive and will allow our mind to 'see' and understand the external environment better.

Social intelligence

This is a new concept of intelligence, and specifically applies to how we relate to others. From the social intelligence perspective there are four basic ways of interacting with the people around us every day:

1 Socially intelligent minds try to ensure that there is a gain for both parties involved, whether personal or professional. It is, for example, the whole or ideal concept of friendship, or the idea of making a good business deal, where both parties gain something (win-win). There is respect, recognition and a desire for mutual growth.

2 The opposite situation occurs when two destructive minds come together, from the social point of view. These are people who allow themselves to be dragged down by negative emotions and cannot control them, and try to psychologically overcome the other person,

when one of the individuals brings into play the worst aspects of their personality. This situation is the opposite of the win-win one: with this attitude both parties end up losing. This is the attitude adopted by couples in the midst of a painful divorce. It is the typical, 'I lose – you lose' situation.

3   An egotistic person will try to take advantage of, or put one over, the other person. In this case one of the parties gains the upper hand at the expense of the other. This type of abusive behaviour needs careful handling, because as you sow, so shall you reap. In this situation the wishes of the other person are not taken into account, only your own. It is an 'I win – you lose' formula.

4   And finally, there are the masochistic people who allow themselves to be dominated by everyone else, completely annihilating their own personality, desires and needs. This situation is the complete opposite of the previous one. It is the same interaction but seen from the weaker side. The formula is: 'I lose – you win'.

Brands, products, services and communications must try to build constructive and gratifying relationships with the consumer, that are clearly within the win-win territory of intelligent mind. But it does not always work that way. Those brands that drift away from this approach will find themselves facing very negative consumer reactions in the future. Figure 8.1 shows these four different relationships, which use very different types of social intelligence.

FIGURE 8.1

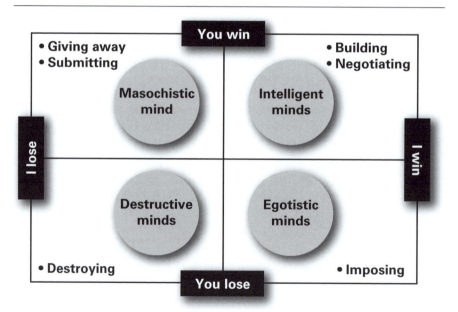

Summary of key learning points about brands

- Brands, products, services and communications must try to build constructive and gratifying relationships with the consumer that seek the best for both parties.

- Because a brand is like a type of 'contract' between two parties – the producer and the consumer – the brand has to fulfil the expectations it has created.

- Intelligent brands are those that look for the best for their consumers, because in this way they create positive experiences that are passed on to others by word of mouth.

- Intelligent brands, good brands, brands with soul, are those that behave like the archetypal good mother: she teaches her children what to eat, what they have to do, what they have to use, what they have to buy but always looking for what is best for her son or daughter (the consumer).

- 'Bad' brands are like the wicked stepmother (they mistreat their children-consumers) or like a witch (they deceive them). They are brands with no soul. They are the negative counterpart of the archetypal good mother.

Who's the boss here?

09

> *"The mind is its own place, and in itself can make a Heaven of Hell, a Hell of Heaven.*
>
> **JOHN MILTON**

The boss

The issue I am going to discuss in this chapter is key to our daily existence. I am going to try to answer the formidable question of who is responsible for managing our life.

We have a body, a brain and a mind, which form a more or less integrated whole that we call 'me' or 'self'. But where is the control tower for this 'self'? Our first response is: in the brain, in the mind. The brain is in charge of managing our body, our daily decisions. The brain, functioning as a whole, carries out this complex mission. However, is there some part of the brain that has a greater role in this management activity? Well, yes. The frontal lobe is the orchestra conductor in our journey through life. I use the word 'conductor' because it needs various sections (of the orchestra) to fulfil its function effectively.

It is possible to create an analogy between the frontal lobe and the managing director of a company. A general manager needs the collaboration of the various departments within the enterprise and needs to synchronize them in order to successfully achieve its goals. If we compare the thought area (frontal lobe) with a general manager, then the language area, and the act of giving or exchanging information and messages with others, could be seen as being equivalent to a company's communications department.

In the case of emotions (feelings, the limbic brain), parallels could be established with the human resources department. If the brain has to move into action, it helps to know how the person feels, their mood. For a general manager, it is essential to understand the working atmosphere within his or her enterprise, such as the level of motivation within the workforce, or their commitment to the company's objectives.

As far as behaviour is concerned, action (the area of doing) is analogous to the commercial, operations or logistics and maintenance departments of a company. The company's technical department would be the equivalent of the brain's frontal lobe (the rational dimension). The structure and functioning of houses, cars and businesses are a projection of the body and the human mind.

The frontal lobe leads the decision-making process, but it has to collaborate with other areas of the brain. For the moment, the frontal lobe is the latest step in the evolutionary development of humans. This is why it is specifically responsible for high level mental functions such as:

- the act of thinking: the cognitive process, using reason;
- planning and executive control;
- problem solving;
- decision making, as we will see in the next chapter;
- consciousness;
- ego (the subject's identity);
- the mind's social dimension: interrelating with others;
- ethical and moral judgement: standards, knowledge, the Freudian superego; and
- a focus on the future: predicting events, anticipating and planning for what is to come.

Level 1 of the brain (doing) is related to the present, and action. Level 2 (feeling) is related to past memory. Level 4 (thought) looks towards the future (reasoning) and anticipates the possible consequences of any action. (Look back to Figure 2.2, which shows all four levels.)

Planning and executive control are complex activities involving different areas of the brain and various mental functions, such as:

- paying attention;
- drawing up a plan of action;
- establishing a sequence of activities focusing on an objective; and
- carrying out a plan of action.

Preparing a plan is relatively simple because most plans do not tend to fail at the diagnosis and conceptual stage, but during the implementation stage. History bears witness to the millions of good intentions that failed to materialize.

The frontal lobe is the 'boss' because it is responsible for coordinating the main areas of the brain in charge of key mental functions. Some of these functions include:

- perception;
- attention;

- memory (working and long-term memory);
- emotions;
- language;
- motor activities (behaviour, actions); sometimes the action might be verbal as thought and language often replace actions; neurones (the nervous system), which are evolutionarily superior to muscles, coordinate almost all the muscular system.

Who governs our daily life and our destiny? The brain is the 'control tower' and the frontal lobe is the 'general manger'.

Who am I?

The evolutionary development of the human mind has reached an amazing achievement: consciousness. The brain is the only organ capable of thinking about itself. The rest of the body's organs cannot achieve this however hard they try. The human brain has transcended the biological and entered into the realms of psychology, sociology, history and philosophy.

All this is thanks to consciousness. Consciousness allows us to think about ourselves, to see ourselves as someone who is different to others and distinct from the environment around us. Consciousness gives us an identity in the world. Our consciousness differentiates us from other people.

Consciousness is the most complex feature of the human mind. Conscious activity is a continuum ranging from the very simple and basic to the very complex and sophisticated:

- vigilant state, waking up, switching on the brain, the arousal state;
- alert state, warning, focusing attention on a dangerous situation;
- concentrating the focus of attention on specific stimuli that acquire relevance as a whole;
- conscious experience, self-awareness, the perception of oneself as being different to others, as someone unique and unrepeatable, with a past, a present and a future (historic dimension); it is the prospect of thinking in the 'then' (the past), and in the 'now' (the present), or in what is to come (the future); it allows for all combinations of time and space variables.

The conscious part of the 'self' is in the brain. For some authors the conscious is particularly linked to frontal lobe activity, which is the latest achievement in the evolutionary development of the human brain. The 'self' would be something like the sum total of long-term memory (LTM) and the direct activity of the frontal lobe. All the experiences we have lived, and that make up our identity, are recorded in our LTM:

self = LTM + frontal lobe

For other writers, consciousness and this concept of 'self' is the result of brain activity as a whole. From this perspective, consciousness arises as a result of the whole brain working as a team. Consciousness appears thanks to the synchronized collaboration of the various areas in the brain (or the nervous system). In this sense, the frontal lobe and LTM are important factors in conscious activity, and are integrated as part of a very complicated whole that includes other areas that also have to be taken into account, and where the whole is more than the sum of the parts.

Consciousness is the capacity to think about ourselves, about others and about the world around us. Consciousness opens the door to the philosophical dimension of life. It allows us to reflect on psychosocial phenomena and on the actions we carry out every day. The more conscious we are about the content and function of our minds, the more capable we will be in drawing up effective action plans for the future.

When there are emotional issues that we are not aware of, these can emerge suddenly and create interference and 'white noise' in our relationship with ourselves and with others. All this will be out of our control because they have escaped the focus of our consciousness. The more aware we are of the issues that are in play in the different situations in our daily life, the more relevant information we have to enable us to draw up more suitable action plans and make better decisions.

The concept of 'self', namely our identity, is something highly complex. What do we mean by this idea of 'self'? Is it the image we have of ourselves, the way we look at ourselves, the person we believe ourselves to be? Is it the image others have of us, the way others see us, the person that others believe us to be?

I would like to spend a moment on a classic model that we might find useful in understanding ourselves, other people and consumers: the Johari window. It is a conceptualization device developed by the psychologists Joseph Luft and Harry Ingham. This model helps us understand the concept of identity and provides a launch pad for discussing personality. The Johari window, shown in Figure 9.1, has four quadrants:

Open zone: refers to that part of every one of us that is known both to the individual and to other people.

Hidden zone: is the area known to the individual but unknown to everyone else. This consists of anything pertaining to the intimacy of the individual.

Blind spot: what is known to everyone else but that our own 'self' is unaware of. It is as if individuals have difficulty in seeing their own façade, to see how they really are, because they are not objective.

The unknown area: which refers to the area that is completely unknown to both the individual and to others.

FIGURE 9.1 Johari 'Window'

Aspects of personality	Known to self	Not known to self
Known to others	Open zone	Blind zone
Not known to others	Hidden zone	Unknown zone

The ideal situation, for both people and brands, is coherence between these four perceptions. The more aware we are of the aspects present in each of these, the better.

Sometimes, within a company, the perception of a brand is very different to the perception on the street (the consumer's point of view). In other cases, consumers have a very different perception of a brand to that of non-consumers. Or we may find different perceptions with different age groups. It is very important that a brand's image is consistent.

The Johari window can be very useful in the workplace for the boss to provide feedback on team members. It is important that this feedback is:

- Applicable to a particular form of behaviour, as specific as possible, and the behaviour should be modifiable.
- Neutral: it is better that the feedback be descriptive, objective and focused on facts, rather than evaluative, subjective and based on interpretation.
- Opportune: finding the best time to give feedback so that it is as constructive as possible and achieves a positive effect. The best time is when the person receiving the feedback is in a position to be the most receptive.
- Direct: in the most personal and close way possible.
- Verified: it is useful to ask the person to sum up what has been said to them to ensure that the message has been conveyed effectively and it has been understood correctly.

Because the human mind is very complex, two further views of a person's identity can be added to the Johari window – the ideal and the real self. The 'ideal self' is the person I would like to be, to which I aspire (my reference framework); this is the idealized image of myself. Then there is the 'real self': the person I am in reality every day (belonging framework).

People with a strong, mature identity have integrated and synchronized all these aspects into one single identity. They have managed to articulate the vision they have of themselves with that of others, matching desire to reality and the conscious dimension with their unconscious aspects. These are people who are engaged in what they do and are true to themselves; they constantly strive to learn more about themselves and others. They are true researchers into their own psychology and interpersonal relationships.

What am I like?

To really understand who we are as individuals or what other people are like, or what the specific typology of a consumer is like, we have to differentiate between the various concepts.

The first of these is the concept of temperament. This refers to the innate disposition that each of us has when we come into this world and which conditions us to react in a certain way when faced with life's events. Temperament is determined genetically. It is closely associated with the body (biological dimension), and relies in particular on the central nervous system and the endocrine system. Temperament has a hereditary component and an impact on emotions. It makes us live life to different degrees of intensity and regulates how much of our emotions we express externally (to others, the environment) or internally (to ourselves).

The second pertinent concept is character. Sometimes the ideas of temperament, character and personality are used interchangeably: they are indeed closely linked but they are different. Character is the dynamic organization of a person's behavioural patterns. By this we mean the reactions and behavioural habits acquired through interacting with the environment, and it is generally formed during the first few years of life (psychological dimension).

Character is like a person's fingerprint. Brands also have character, and vice versa: character brands them in a specific way. If we go back to the origins of the word 'brand' it takes us to the practice of branding cattle to distinguish them from the neighbour's herd. The noun 'brand' is German in origin and comes from the verb meaning to burn or mark with fire. So, character brands us.

The third is personality. Personality is the integration of temperament (genetic and hereditary dimension) and character (acquired and environmental dimension). Personality is a dynamic concept that explains the way we react and relate to the environment around us in the multitude of situations life throws at us. Personality is a type of set pattern and equates, more or less, to temperament plus character. The formula would be:

personality = temperament + character

An individual's personality depends greatly on the specific role or relative weight given to each of the mind's four basic software programs:

1 thought (thinking);
2 emotions (feeling);
3 communication (listening and speaking); and
4 action (doing).

Mature people have achieved their character through using each of these four mental functions sufficiently and have achieved a high level of integration and synchronization between all of them. On the other hand, there are individuals who tend to favour one of these functions at the expense of the others. For example, an obsessive person almost always resorts to the thought process; they think excessively and in a way that is disconnected from their emotions.

Hysterical personalities are basically supported by their feelings and live life in an extreme fashion. They are characterized by their great emotional intensity. These feelings tend to be fairly unattached to the thought process. On the other hand, impulsive personalities tend towards action. They act without prior reflection (thought) and their behaviour tends to be largely determined by their emotions.

Our personality determines to a great extent the role each of these four basic dimensions – thinking, feeling, communicating and acting – have acquired in our lives. In turn, the combination of these four activities determines how we are in the world, how we interact with others and with ourselves, our behaviour and the relationship we have with brands, products and services.

Consumer discussions in focus groups or during in-depth interviews may or may not integrate these traits. Sometimes we find great internal cohesion, but on other occasions consumers say what they think and do what they feel. This is when the moderator has to resort to interpreting their meaning to fully understand what is going on in the consumer's mind.

Brands have to be consistent in what they say because their credibility is at stake. Credibility is a key factor for modern consumers. All the active areas relating to a brand (thinking, feeling, communicating and doing) have to be consistent with its spirit and its values and they have to be properly synchronized. A brand's marketing mix (concept, name, image, product, packaging, labelling, communications, offers, distribution and price) have to be coherent, original and different to the competition; they also have to be attractive to consumers and motivate them. Market segmentation studies have shown that personality has a huge influence on lifestyle and the consumer.

Summary of key learning points about brands

- The 'Johari window' shows us four areas of interest to brands:
  - Open quadrant: known to the brand and known to others (consumers and competitors).
  - Hidden quadrant: known to the company, but not to everyone else; for example, the brand's strategy.
  - Blind quadrant: known to others, but not to the brand in question. Sometimes there are perceptions on the street or new views of the brand, positive or negative, that the company does not know about.
  - Unknown quadrant: to the brand, to consumers and to competitors. This may be new trends that are emerging and that may create changes within the category and the brand in question.

- It is very beneficial to the brand's strategy to know as much as possible about these four areas; and it is crucial that the brand's image is original, attractive and consistent.

- Brands have to be consistent in what they say because their credibility is at stake. Credibility is a key factor for modern consumers.

- All the active areas relating to a brand (thinking, feeling, communicating and doing) have to be consistent with its spirit and its values and they have to be properly synchronized.

- A brand's marketing mix (concept, name, image, product, packaging, labelling, communications, offers, distribution and price) have to be coherent, original and different to the competition; they also have to be attractive to consumers and motivate them.

Make your mind up!

10

> *The firefly only shines when on the wing;*
> *so is it with the mind.*   **BAILEY**

A long cultural tradition

We have grown up in a western culture, where great importance is placed on the rational aspects of being human. This is logical if we consider that the ability to think is the fundamental difference between humans and other species of animals.

Until the beginning of the 19th century it was thought that human behaviour was guided, or ought to be guided, by thought or by reason. But towards the end of the 18th and beginning of the 19th centuries, the theories of Sigmund Freud (1856–1939) showed that our behaviour can be greatly influenced by unconscious issues relating to emotions stored within the mind, to which we do not have access from the conscious mind.

If we consult the *Oxford English Dictionary,* we find the following definition for 'human being': 'a man or woman, or child of the species "Homo sapiens".' Sapiens means 'wise', defined as: 'having or showing experience, knowledge and good judgement'. This highlights the human traits of wisdom, knowledge and reasoning. This is echoed by the Spanish equivalent of the *OED*, the *Diccionario de la Real Academia de la Lengua Española*, where the word *hombre* (man – in the sense of human species) is defined as a 'rational being, male or female'. There is no reference to the difficulties humans have in marrying the rational world with the emotional world.

It would probably be more correct to say that humans constitute a species that strives to reason; they do what they can. Sometimes they try to reason, but can't handle their emotions: they overwhelm them. Sometimes they do manage to use reason. And sometimes they think they are trying to be reasonable, but they only manage to be rational.

Let's go back, in our imagination, to Ancient Greece, to meet the Greek philosopher Plato (428 or 427 BC to 347 BC). He was a disciple of Socrates and master to Aristotle. These three men could be seen as the builders of the pillars of current thinking in western society.

Plato espoused the idea of anthropological dualism, where humans have two halves: the body, belonging to the visible world, is the sensible dimension, the material reality – this includes emotions, given that this dualism has a clear correlation to biology and physiology; and the soul, which belongs to the invisible dimension, the world of ideas, the divine essence, and is characterized by its immortality. The soul was the main aspect for Plato, enclosed in its corporeal prison; its purpose is to do good in this life and to free itself from the body at the end of the journey.

Plato's idea of duality was taken up by St Augustine (354–430). Augustine of Hippo adapted Plato's ideas to the Christian doctrine. In book VIII of his Confessions he clearly showed a dichotomy between the body – the material life, bodily pleasures and earthly life; and the soul – the spiritual life. We can already see the struggle between forces pulling in opposite directions. We can see that humans are not just rational beings, but individuals made up of an ensemble of very different possibilities.

This cultural tradition we have inherited gives greater importance to the soul, the rational dimension of humans, to their capacity for thinking and the force of reason. All this was to the detriment of bodily needs, emotions and satisfying desires. This is why our culture does not look favourably on emotions, because they have always been loaded with negative connotations. Emotions have been, and still are, something dangerous to be controlled and even repressed. The arrival of Freud changed that somewhat. He demonstrated that being human is not about being totally rational, and that emotions and inconsistency influence a person's behaviour and determine the path he or she takes in life.

Everything seems to indicate that we have two minds in one body: a rational mind (the prefrontal lobe), and an emotional mind (the limbic brain). The emotional mind is much more closely linked to the body. Plato, St Augustine, Descartes, Freud and a host of other writers had understood this.

These two areas of the brain are connected: emotions are born in the limbic brain, and are felt in the prefrontal lobe. But on many occasions we find that these two areas have problems agreeing. Daniel Goleman, in his book *Emotional Intelligence*, arrived at some interesting conclusions on this phenomenon:

> Still, the emotional and rational minds are semi-independent faculties, each, as we shall see, reflecting the operation of distinct, but interconnected circuitry in the brain.
>
> The emotional/rational dichotomy approximates the folk distinction between 'heart' and 'head'; knowing something is 'right in your heart' is a different order of conviction – somehow a deeper kind of certainty – than thinking with your rational mind.

In this last paragraph we see that Daniel Goleman gives greater importance to the emotions. He is trying to put things in their rightful place after so many years of reason having the primary position. As we shall see later, reason and emotion are a necessary binomial expression and complement each other in good decision making.

Descartes' Error

Antonio Damasio is a Portuguese doctor and neurologist. He was born in Lisbon in 1944. He is an expert in the neurology of behaviour and in analysing the neurological basis of the mind. Together with his wife, he received the Prince of Asturias prize in 2005 for scientific and technological research. He is the author of several books:

1994, *Descartes' Error: Emotion, reason, and the human brain* nominated for the *Los Angeles Times* Book Award.

2001, *The Feeling of What Happens: Body and emotion in the making of consciousness* was considered a top 10 book by the *New York Times* Book Review.

2003, *Looking for Spinoza: Joy, sorrow and the feeling brain.*

The philosopher René Descartes (1596–1650) was born in La Haye en Touraine, France, and is considered the father of modern philosophy. He outlined his philosophy during a period known as the Rationalist era in continental Europe, when great importance was given to rationalism. Once again emotions were relegated to second place.

Descartes inherited this dualistic way of thinking, clearly distinguishing between *res extensa,* the body, and *res cogitans,* the soul. For Descartes the body and soul were totally different matters. He chose to follow the *res cogitans.* The 'self' is related to the soul, and to the mind. However, if dualism is extended further in this direction, and the soul is said to be present throughout the body, there is a place where the connection is made: the brain, specifically the pineal gland. This is the view championed by Damasio in *Descartes' Error.* Here are some illustrative paragraphs from this well-known book:

> I had been advised early in life that sound decisions came from a cool head, that emotions and reason did not mix any more than oil and water.
>
> The main subject in *Descartes' Error* is the relation between emotion and reason. Based upon my study of neurological patients who had both defects of decision-making and a disorder of emotions, I advanced the hypothesis (known as the somatic-marker hypothesis) that emotion was in the loop of reason, and that emotion could assist the reasoning process rather than necessarily disturb it, as was commonly presumed.
>
> The new proposal in *Descartes Error* is that the reasoning system evolved as an extension of the automatic emotional system, with emotion playing diverse roles in the reasoning process.

Never does reasoning act alone, and that is the key point put forward in *Descartes' Error*. When emotion is entirely left out of the reasoning picture, as happens in certain neurological conditions, reason turns out to be even more flawed than when emotion plays bad tricks on our decisions.

The somatic-marker hypothesis postulated from the start that emotions marked certain aspects of a situation, or certain outcomes of possible actions. Emotion achieved this marking quite overtly, as in a 'gut feeling', or covertly, via signals occurring below the radar of our awareness. As for the knowledge used in reasoning, it too could be fairly explicit or partially hidden, as when we intuit a solution. In other words, emotion had a role to play in intuition, the sort of rapid cognitive process in which we came to a particular conclusion without being aware of all the immediate logical steps.

Emotions can be really helpful in the decision-making process. The use of cold and calculated reasoning alone in the thought process can lead us to make grave mistakes when taking important decisions in our lives.

Antonio Damasio's somatic-marker concept is very useful when we have to make a decision. It refers to the whole ensemble of physical and emotional traces, positive or negative valences, which act on every one of us (according to our personal history) when faced with a specific situation, and that can help us to take a specific decision.

The conclusion we are going to reach here is that the best decisions in our lives are those that have emerged from a good collaboration between reasoning and emotion, between the prefrontal lobe and the limbic brain (the 'reason-emotion binomial'). Descartes divided humans into two parts (dualism) and gave the greater role to reasoning (rationalism), skimming over the role played by the emotions. He did not consider that emotions could even generate background noise in the thought process.

Looking for Spinoza

The philosopher Spinoza (1632–1677) lived just after the Descartes period. Spinoza was born in Amsterdam to a family originally from Portugal. He was another of the distinguished philosophers from the Rationalist period, but his view diverged from Descartes' (Cartesian), dualist view.

Spinoza established a continuum between the body, the mind and the world (nature). He reclaimed physical emotions and incorporated them as a very important part of being human. He called them 'affects'. Damasio shares very similar views to Spinoza (as he outlines in his book *Looking for Spinoza*) and moves away from Descartes' focus.

Spinoza had a holistic view of the person, a 360-degree panorama in which he referred to the function of our mind. There is a highly interrelated continuity between our body, our psychology and the world around us. We cannot deny the rhetoric of the body, nor the emotions, because that would mean renouncing a very significant part of our nature.

In his book *Descartes' Error*, Damasio notes:

> Surprising as it may sound, the mind exists in and for an integrated organism; our minds would not be the way they are if it were not for the interplay of body and brain during evolution, during individual development, and at the current moment.

Later, in *Looking for Spinoza,* he explains why it is important to focus on this philosopher and to reclaim his way of thinking:

> Spinoza saw drives, motivations, emotions and feelings – an ensemble Spinoza called 'affects' – as a central aspect of humanity.
>
> Spinoza dealt with the subjects that preoccupy me most as a scientist – the nature of emotions and feelings and the relation of mind to body ... his notion that both the mind and the body were parallel attributes (call them manifestations) of the very same substance.

The rational-emotional binomial

After that brief run through the history of thought, we have reached the point where we discover the importance of reason and emotion in the decision-making process.

The evolution of humankind, from our closest ancestors, has generated and added new layers and areas to the brain, which, in turn, has allowed new mental functions to appear: action, emotion, communication (language) and thought. At the same time, this growth has required the different functions to collaborate with each other. The human mind is a result of teamwork.

Javier Tirapu, in his book *¿Para qué sirve el cerebro? (manual para principiantes)* (What is the brain for? A manual for beginners), gives this comprehensive view of the human mind:

> The balance between the rational mind (frontal lobe) and the emotional mind (limbic system) is found by understanding how it functions in order to be able to control it, and, consequently, to use it for our own benefit.
>
> In the brain the reasoning processes (cognition-knowledge) and the emotions should unite to indicate the correct path for us to take.
>
> Antonio Damasio's somatic-marker hypothesis should be understood as a theory intended to explain the role of the emotions in reasoning and decision making.
>
> In the extreme of the hippocampus (memory store) is a small structure known as the amygdala, which is closely related to emotional learning and with fear in particular. Therefore, we can state that there is a cold, calculating system which stores information about the world (hippocampus) and a burning, passionate system which gathers emotional information (amygdala). Under normal conditions both systems work in coordination, as the hippocampus gathers information and the context in which it is produced, the amygdala does the same for the emotional aspects.

The ideal is a balance between thought and emotions. If we make a decision based solely on our reasoning, it may not be the decision we like the best or the one best suited to our personality. If we make a decision based only on our emotions, we will have to choose the option with which we feel most comfortable, or that pleases us the most, but it may not be the best route for us. When we have to make a decision, we ought to work through the following steps:

1 Think openly about the possible scenarios emerging before us. Try to have a fairly open brainstorming session and mentally outline the various possibilities. This involves using imagination and creativity.

2 Rationally analyse the advantages and disadvantages to each of these scenarios (the frontal lobe, which tries to analyse the external reality).

3 Project ourselves onto each of the situations to see how we feel emotionally; gauging the level of attractiveness when thinking of ourselves, of what we like and what we don't like (the limbic system, which tries to analyse our internal world). By doing this we can give different weights to each of the scenarios.

This is why not everyone chooses the same option. There is probably more resemblance in the rational analysis of the advantages and disadvantages of each scenario, but personal projection onto each of these situations changes greatly depending on the individual's somatic marker.

The relationship between the frontal lobe and the limbic brain is a type of electrical system composed of two wires. The wire that goes from the emotional system to the frontal lobe is thicker, solid and powerful, while the wire that runs in the opposite direction is thinner, flimsy and weak. This is why emotions have such a strong effect and so much influence on thoughts. It is much harder to control emotions from reasoning. The negotiations between reason and emotions are a matter of daily practice and use.

If we use the analogy of a car, we can say that the accelerator (the connection between the limbic system and the prefrontal lobe) works better than the brake (counter connection, which connects the prefrontal cortex and the limbic brain). Figure 10.1 shows the location of the frontal lobe and the limbic system within the brain. Decision making should be a collaborative interplay between these two areas.

The frontal lobe is associated with reasoning, will, control, inhibiting certain behaviours, the principle of reality, and with being able to postpone rewards with a view to the medium and long term. The limbic brain is associated with emotions, impulses, a person's addictive side, immediate gratification, and with the principle of pleasure with a view to the short term (immediacy).

Continuing with the metaphor of a car: good driving means using the accelerator and the brake appropriately. Both are necessary, but they need to be used skilfully in line with the nature of the road, which symbolizes the external circumstances, the reality that surrounds us.

FIGURE 10.1

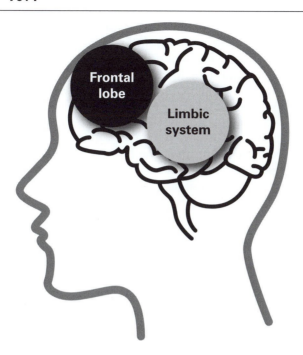

A person may have multiple addictive aspects to his or her nature, but they may not be extreme or serious. Depending on their different cultures, people may be addicted to or really dislike sweets, coffee, cola drinks, smoking, alcohol, eating meat and not fish, etc. Javier Tirapu puts it like this:

> We know that connections running from the cortical areas (reasoning) to the nucleus of the amygdala are much weaker than those running in the opposite direction to the cortex; therefore, it is very easy for emotions to control our thoughts and so costly when thoughts reduce our emotions to compliance with reason.

For Damasio, emotion is faster and comes first. Thought is a little slower and arrives later. Personally, I really like the research described by Daniel Goleman in *Emotional Intelligence*. It is a study carried out at Stanford University on four-year-olds, the children of professors, employees and students at the university. This is how Goleman explained it:

> Just imagine you're four years old, and someone makes the following proposal: if you'll wait until after he runs an errand, you can have two marshmallows for a treat. If you can't wait until then, you can have only one – but you can have it right now. It is a challenge sure to try the soul of any four-year-old, a microcosm of the eternal battle between impulse and restraint, id and ego, desire and self-control, gratification and delay.

It is a really difficult exercise for children because they have to repress their impulses, which are very strong at 4 years old. Those who manage to succeed show huge emotional control. These children have understood that the wait is worthwhile, and they will receive double the pleasure (two marshmallows) in 20 minutes (return on investment).

This is how the frontal lobe inhibits impulses from the limbic brain, as a secondary process overriding the first process, as the reality principle leapfrogs over the pleasure principle and as will manages to tame emotions. These subjects successfully negotiated with their emotions and managed to postpone them to later achieve twice the gratification.

As we have seen, it is not about repressing or denying emotions. It is about learning to negotiate with them. The objective of the 'self' is to draw up contracts between the emotions, desires, impulses and external reality.

These same children were studied again during their teenage years, and it was seen that those who had managed to wait 20 minutes to receive two marshmallows instead of one were:

> more socially competent: personally effective, self-assertive, and better able to cope with the frustrations of life. They were less likely to go to pieces, freeze, or regress under stress, or become rattled and disorganized when pressured; they embraced challenges and pursued them instead of giving up even in the face of difficulties; they were self-reliant and confident, trustworthy and dependable; and they took the initiative and plunged into projects. And, more than a decade later, they were still able to delay gratification in pursuit of their goals.

In Greek culture, the god Apollo represented stability, recognizing one's own abilities, formal questions and balance (frontal lobe, rational mind). On the other hand, Dionysus (Bacchus to the Romans) symbolized values associated at that time with wine: ritual frivolity, excess and hedonism (the limbic brain, the emotional mind).

The consumer and decision making

This dynamic between the frontal lobe and the limbic system is present every day in the decisions we consumers make with regard to consuming brands, products or services.

Let us think about the food we consume every day. The rational aspect of our mind pushes us towards duties, towards rules, towards what is best for us in the medium and long term, towards the reality principle (Freud), etc. The frontal lobe, the thought area, analyses the consequences of ingesting various foodstuffs. This way, we know the ideal is to eat vegetables, fruit and fish. We know that a good diet is one that is balanced, one that contains a little of everything.

The frontal lobe brings to the forefront that we must think about the health of our body and the aesthetic dimension. If we want to be healthy and attractive the best thing we can do is eat food that is low in fat and will not make us gain weight. The rational mind does not look for immediate gratification, but makes us think of the medium- and long-term consequences. This is what Freud called the secondary process or reality principle.

The emotional and impulsive mind opts for immediate satisfaction in the short term, the pleasure principle and the primary process (Freud), enjoyment, pleasure, etc. It is about succumbing to the oral pleasure offered by specific foods.

This is when a dynamic tussle begins in our brains between the rational mind and the emotional mind. We want to be healthy and attractive (prefrontal lobe), but we are attracted to sweets (limbic brain). Looking after oneself is good for your health, but it is boring, it requires a lot of discipline and effort from us.

The same happens when it comes to doing exercise, such as going out and running for half an hour every day. Doing sport is good for the body (health and keeping in shape). However, it involves a major effort and being disciplined. Once again we feel that tension between forces pulling in opposite directions. It is a type of dialogue between two very different people within our minds, the worker and the *bon viveur*.

If we think of an executive who has to travel from Madrid to Barcelona, and the way in which he or she assesses the various options when preparing the journey, by plane, by train (high speed), by coach or by car. Many people are afraid of flying; it creates negative emotions for them (insecurity, anxiety, distress). The limbic system (amygdala) is activated by the simple fact that they have thought about taking a plane.

However, if we analyse the situation from the prefrontal lobe, the view is very different because air travel is the safest mode of transport there is. Statistics favour taking the plane. The risk of suffering an accident is much higher if you take the car or travel by coach. But in this case it is very likely that emotions will win over reason and fear of flying will overcome statistics (logical and rational dimensions). As a matter of fact, the high speed rail service between Madrid and Barcelona works very successfully. The train avoids the negative feelings associated with flying, the risk of having an accident is also fairly low, the service is very good, customers enjoy much more personal space and it is reasonably quick.

If we listen to a conversation between executives about the advantages and disadvantages of travelling by plane or high speed train, we will definitely be able to identify many good reasons and strong emotions, and fairly rational suggestions that cover up these emotions. In consumer discussions on brands, products and services, a mixture of reasons, emotions and rationalizations always emerge. Our task as researchers is to clearly identify them, to classify them and understand how they interrelate, in order for the consumer to take that final decision.

Reason must not be confused with rationalization. Rationalization is the defence mechanism used to hide from ourselves the true intentions behind our actions. Emotion is first, reason comes after. A particular consumer may be wrapped up in the decision-making process for purchasing a car. Emotions nudge him towards a BMW, probably because of the status and sporty image associated with the brand, or for the simple pleasure of driving. But the potential buyer's argument is to tell himself that it is a car he really needs because it is very safe and roomy.

Rationalization is a psychological defence mechanism that consists of justifying actions carried out by the subject themselves. It is a type of explanation that adopts the appearance of logic, but hides the true emotions, feelings and behaviour of the person in question.

These internal dialogues very often produce different scenes in our daily lives. The final decisions we make depend on the strength of the personalities acting in our minds. One personality represents will, the voice of the conscience, Jiminy Cricket ... while the other represents the hedonist.

A mature and integrated mind establishes a dialogue between the various areas of the brain (mental functions) and finally chooses the option that most benefits the person in the medium or long term (secondary process, reality principle). A fragmented, disassociated mind shows a lack of coherence in its decision-making process, since it makes decisions haphazardly, depending largely on the personality that is taking the lead role at that particular time.

The Transactional Analysis model (put forward by Eric Berne, Canadian doctor and psychiatrist, 1910–1970) is a North American development and adaptation of the psychoanalytic perspective, and offers three 'personalities' or authorities within our mind:

1 The 'Parent' (which represents rules, duties, Freud's Super-ego).
2 The 'Child' (impulses, desires, the Freudian Id).
3 And the 'Adult' (who has to manage the demands of the 'Parent' and the 'Child' and connect them with the external reality). It corresponds to Freud's Ego.

These three 'personalities' are present in the 'theatre' of our mind. Sometimes we think, feel, speak and behave in the role of the 'Parent' (authority). At other times, in the role of the 'Child', we get carried away by our impulses and desires, letting our most basic emotional reactions assert themselves.

The ideal seems to be to take on the personality of the 'Adult', which is the most mature and constructive of the three. It is the one that best reconciles rules and desires with the external reality. The specific weighting each of these three personalities has within our mind determines our personality, our way of being and our way of behaving. Every now and again it is advisable to carry out a self-analysis of our various actions throughout the day to see how these personalities are evolving in our mind and to identify what areas are being left to the 'Adult'.

Advertising campaigns, reasoning and emotions

At Millward Brown we analysed 330 advertising 'spots' in our communication pretest database (Link methodology). For these 330 ads, we knew the communications impact on sales. We have categorized these 330 communications into three strategy groups:

1 rational;

2 emotional; and

3 combined.

Figure 10.2 shows us that in all these cases (all the brands, big and small) the use of a combined strategy (emotions plus reasoning) had the most positive effect on sales. This confirms that a good combination of reasoning and emotions tends to work successfully, in life and in advertising.

FIGURE 10.2

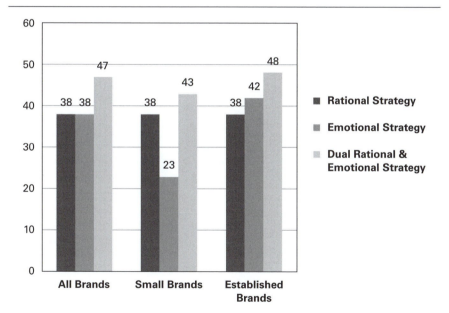

Summary of key learning points about brands

- In discussions with consumers on brands, products and services, a mixture of reasons, emotions and rationalizations always emerge. Our task as researchers is to clearly identify these, to classify them and understand how they interrelate.

- Reason must not be confused with rationalization. Rationalization is the defence mechanism used to hide from ourselves the true intentions behind our actions.

- A brand has to connect with the relevant, positive emotions in consumers ('reasons to believe') and, at the same time, to give them good reasons to use the brand ('reasons why').

- The analysis of the 330 advertising 'spots' in our database showed us that using a combined communications strategy (reasoning plus emotions) had a more positive effect on the sales of the product or service being advertised.

- A good combination of reasoning and emotions tends to work successfully, in life and in advertising.

I want to be happy!

11

> **"** *Men continually forget that happiness is a condition of mind and not a disposition of circumstances.* JOHN LOCKE

The illusion of happiness

Everyone is looking for happiness. Our goal in life is to be happy: happiness is like the Holy Grail or the Philosopher's Stone. The main questions to be answered are: what are we really looking for, and where are we looking for it?

When we try to achieve happiness we may find that many illusions or mirages appear on the way. We are going to focus on the main ones:

- something material;
- fame or success in life;
- something major that might happen to us;
- something that comes from without;
- luck, fortune or chance;
- something that might or might not arrive, so you have to wait;
- something that when it does arrive, stays forever;
- something that the people around us have to give us;
- something that has to do with the more advanced countries (United States, Western Europe, Japan, etc).

We are going to pause at each of these 'mirages' and dispel them to find the real 'oasis' of happiness.

The first of these shows us happiness directly related to the material world; for example, having a lot of money, winning the lottery, physical beauty, having a nice body, being able to travel extensively, having the opportunity to take a cruise, etc. But really happiness is not about the material. Happiness is not about satisfying a person's every need and desire:

Don't mistake pleasure for happiness. They are a different breed of dogs.
(Josh Billings)

Real happiness is not costly. If it is dear, then it's the wrong kind.
(Francois R Chateaubriand)

Having everything to be happy, is in no way reason to be so.
(Jacques Normand)

Wealth consists not in having great possessions, but in having few
wants.   (Epictetus)

Desire and happiness cannot live together.   (Epictetus)

The superior man loves his soul; the inferior man loves his possessions.
(Lin Yutang)

Very little is needed to make a happy life.   (Marcus Aurelius)

To be without some of the things you want is an indispensable part of
happiness.   (Bertrand Russell)

The fewer our wants the more we resemble the Gods.   (Socrates)

Happiness is not needing it.   (Seneca)

The second illusion relates happiness with achieving success or fame. Fame
or success does not guarantee happiness; in fact it tends to be the reverse:
happiness brings success or fame. Doing what one enjoys most is the most
likely way of achieving success: 'Success is getting what you want; happiness
is wanting what you get' (Anonymous).

Happiness can also be seen as something major and wonderful turning
up, that comes from outside and suddenly changes our life. On the contrary:
happiness is found in the small but very important details that emerge
around us:

Happiness consists more in the small conveniences or pleasures that
occur every day, than in great pieces of good fortune that happen but
seldom to a man in the course of his life.   (Benjamin Franklin)

Many people lose the small joys in hoping for the big happiness.
(Pearl S Buck)

Happiness is never grand.   (Aldous Huxley)

Very little is needed to make a happy life.   (Marcus Aurelius)

There is happiness to be found in everything, but it is up to each one of
us to extract it.   (Marcus Aurelius)

The less one notices happiness, the greater it is.   (Alberto Moravia)

A great obstacle to happiness is to expect too much happiness.
(Bernard le Bouvier de Fontenelle)

Happiness consists of valuing what you have.   (Helen Keller)

Happiness is not something that comes from without. Happiness is within each one of us, inside our minds. Happiness is the interplay between the external reality (the world around us, other people) and the internal reality (our subjectivity). If we are not looking inside ourselves, we are looking in the wrong place: 'A person who seeks outward happiness is like a snail constantly wandering in search of his home' (Constancio C Vigil).

Happiness is not a question of luck, a stroke of fortune or chance. Happiness is a matter of discipline. It has to be built every day. Happiness demands strength of will, effort, commitment and work. As the popular saying has it: 'There are those who seek out happiness whilst others create it.'

There is also a tendency to think that happiness is something that can happen to me one day, and this creates a state of passive waiting. However, happiness is something you have to look for proactively. Happiness is a certain attitude to life:

> The gift of happiness belongs to those who unwrap it.   (Anonymous)

> It isn't your position in life, it's your disposition that determines your happiness.   (John G Pollard)

> Happiness is not a station you arrive at, but a manner of travelling.   (Margaret L Runbeck)

> The true revolutionary revolutionizes himself.   (Wittgenstein)

Another popular line of thinking is that happiness is something that comes to you one fine day and stays forever. Think, for example, about children's stories set in the world of imagination and fantasy. The stories usually begin with the words, 'Once upon a time ...', and tend to end with the phrase, 'And they lived happily ever after.'

There are also many movies that show or imply a stable and lasting happy ending when the words 'The End' appear on the screen. But happiness does not work in the way it appears in our imagination or fantasies. Happiness is more like an unstable balancing act that has to be calibrated on a daily basis:

> When happiness comes to us, it is never dressed as we thought it should be.   (Madame Amiel-Lapeyre)

> Happiness is like a crystal glass that breaks just at the moment it makes the most beautiful sound.   (Arabic proverb)

It is also thought that happiness consists in receiving many things from others, these things may be material (gifts, money, etc) or immaterial (attention, affection, recognition, etc). But, paradoxically, happiness is quite the opposite; it is about being attentive to others:

> There is only one way to be happy: live for others.   (Leo Tolstoy)

> Happiness is making others happy.   (Francois Lelord)

The secret to happiness is giving rather than receiving.

(Louise M Normand)

The only happiness that we can have comes from the happiness that
    we give.   (Édouard Pailleron)

Happiness: the more you use, the more you have.

(Ralph W Emerson)

Thousands of candles can be lit from a single candle, and the life of
    the candle will not be shortened. Happiness never decreases
    by being shared.   (Buddha)

Happiness tends to be related directly to countries that are more advanced
socio-economically. These issues need to be treated very carefully. There are
many happiness indexes for various countries, and obviously the results
are very different according to the variables taken into account when drawing up these analyses. But the majority of this research agrees in stating
that, paradoxically, the richest, most industrialized countries do not tend
to be the happiest. Therefore, a society's economic and technological development does not run in parallel with the psychological well-being it
generates.

On Google you can find various indexes and classifications for happiness,
by country for example. It all depends on the variables taken into account
when carrying out the analysis. These indexes include the Happiness Index,
Facebook's happiness thermometer, the idea of Gross National Happiness,
or Coca-Cola's Happiness Barometer, among others.

Coca-Cola set up its Happiness Institute and, in conjunction with
Millward Brown, carried out a study on happiness in 16 countries around
the world. Spain ranks number two in Europe, behind Romania. For the
Spanish, the keys to happiness are friends, partners and family. The main
message being communicated currently by Coca-Cola in Spain is '125 años
repartiendo felicidad' (125 years of spreading happiness).

Illusions of happiness confuse us and make us look for the wrong things
in the wrong places. The concept of happiness is very complicated. Let's
look back for a second to ancient Greece, to the oracle of Delphi, and the
temple dedicated to the god Apollo. People came from all over to learn
about their future. Deep down, what they really wanted to know was
whether they would be happy or not. Inscribed above the entrance to the
temple is the maxim: 'Know thyself.' This is where the true secret of our happiness lies. It is within each one of us. We have to look for it there. Happiness
consists in really knowing what we think, how we feel, what we say (clear
and effective communication), and what we do. If there is coherence between these four mental functions, there is every chance we will be happy.
Happy people do and say what they think and feel.

Happiness consists in understanding our needs, our desires and our
expectations. If we are capable of understanding these, then we can adjust
appropriately:

We cannot choose our external circumstances,
but we can always choose how to respond to them. (Epictetus)

It is not easy to find happiness in ourselves,
and it is not possible to find it elsewhere. (Agnes Repplier)

Happiness is closely linked to the difference between our expectations and what we actually achieve. This gap, which can be quite large, is somewhat similar to what occurs with customer satisfaction in consuming or using a product or service. Customers' level of satisfaction will depend on what they expect and the quality they perceive. Satisfaction with a product or service depends on how closely linked the real product or service is to the expected quality.

Therefore, to achieve happiness it is essential to know yourself inside out and to adjust your expectations to your life, your environment and the relationships you have with others. The famous philosopher José Ortega y Gasset tells us that, 'the formula for a happy life has hardly changed throughout human existence'.

Happiness from the psychological point of view

So far we have looked at the myths of happiness. Now let's turn to the keys that can reveal the formula for happiness. Achieving happiness involves the following:

- Being happy with yourself.
- Knowing yourself well.
- A balance between the past, present and future.
- Personal fulfilment through work.
- Being an optimistic realist.
- Having overcome difficulties in life.
- Having goals to achieve.
- Emotional intelligence.
- Looking after the people around you.

The first key to happiness refers to the individual themselves. Happiness is being happy with the person you are. This means accepting yourself. In this sense, happiness is directly related to self-esteem: 'The summit of happiness is reached when a person is ready to be what he is' (Erasmus).

The ideal is to have a good level of self-esteem, neither too high, nor too low. Good self-esteem has to do with an accurate dose of self-assessment. This regulatory mechanism influences happiness. Having good self-esteem brings us close to the concept of happiness. Having too much self-esteem can make a person high-handed and narcissistic. A lack of self-esteem is associated with immaturity and insecurity. But someone with either an excess or a lack of self-esteem can come across as hungry to be recognized by others.

Positive self-esteem is mainly to do with security, confidence, having achieved goals, having a good identity, maturity, personality and strength. A good level of self-esteem is a solid structure for personality, on which personal life, family life, life as a couple and professional life hinge. It is the basis or sturdy foundation on which who we are, and the relationship we have with others, is built. Good self-esteem is a guarantee; it is the best insurance for life.

Happiness also has to do with knowing yourself well – really understanding our thoughts, our emotions (feelings), what we communicate to others and what we do. There has to be coherence between these four levels in our mind. This means we are being true and faithful to the very essence of our being. Mahatma Gandhi said that, 'Happiness is when what you think, what you say, and what you do are in harmony.' I would add to this, 'what you feel' (the emotional dimension).

Happiness is about integrating our past, living life to the full in the present and looking to the future. Everything about happiness is a question of balance. If we are stuck in the past, we will find it difficult to live fully in the present and to be prepared for the future.

Another ingredient in the recipe for happiness is personal fulfilment through the work we do. It is important that we like our occupation, that we project ourselves through it, and that it fills us with passion and enthusiasm. When our work is fulfilling it helps us grow psychologically; our mind feels great benefits. Passion and enthusiasm are contagious:

> Find happiness in your work or you will never be happy.
>
> (Christopher Columbus)

> The secret of happiness is not doing what one likes, but in liking what one does.   (Jean-Paul Sartre)

> The true secret of happiness lies in demanding much of yourself and very little of others.   (Albert Guinon)

> There is only happiness where there is high intention and sincere effort, because life is not a game of chance.   (Aristotle)

For Sigmund Freud, happiness revolves around the ideas of work and love. I would like to highlight a phrase from Freud that helps us to think of the importance of overcoming difficulties to be able to reach happiness: 'I've been a very fortunate man: nothing in my life came easily.'

Erich Fromm believes there are two types of personalities, those who are guided by the concept of having and those by the concept of being. For Fromm, happiness has to do with the idea of 'being':

> The greatest happiness is to transform one's feelings into action.
>
> (Madame de Staël)

> Happiness is inward, and not outward; and so, it does not depend on what we have, but on what we are.   (Henry van Dyke)

Being a realist also helps to achieve happiness, because realism means adjusting our expectations to different situations: 'The happy man is the man who lives objectively' (Bertrand Russell). The optimistic realist is the person closest to happiness. This involves intelligent optimism.

Idealism is dangerous. You have to be careful building castles in the air or being too much of a dreamer. This can lead to nasty surprises. At the same time, pessimism does not allow you to enjoy life because it concentrates excessively on the negative side of reality. On the other hand, being a conformist does not favour the development of one's own identity.

The key is in optimistic realism, because it is linked to:

- Activity, energy and strength.
- Being extrovert and sociable.
- Joy and enjoyment.
- Having initiative, courage, goals and not being afraid.
- Overcoming difficulties.
- And with self-esteem, confidence in one's self.

The secret to my happiness is to treat disasters as if they were nuisances
and not to treat nuisances as if they were disasters. (André Maurois)

A merry heart doeth good like a medicine: but a broken spirit drieth
the bones. (Solomon)

Contrary to what many people think, happiness is having being through difficulties in life and having had the ability to overcome them. This is how a strong, energetic and enthusiastic character is forged, full of hope and a desire to change things that are not working out.

Happiness is also having goals in life. The ideal is that these goals should be attainable and progressive. This way effort will be seen to be rewarded and it will create more energy to reach new goals. Intentions and goals speak of movement, progress, hope and motivation. Goals are synonymous with life and psychological growth. The concept of 'no goals' points in the opposite direction: stagnation, routine, disillusion and depression. 'No goals' is synonymous with death on the psychological level. But if we analyse a person's intentions or goals, we realize that their relationship with happiness depends on many factors:

- Age or the stage an individual is at in their life cycle.
- The significance the goal acquires for this person, ie the way they live their goal (whether it is something very important or of secondary importance, something that requires a lot of commitment, rigidly or with some flexibility, etc).
- The type of goal: big versus small, specific versus abstract, material versus self-fulfilment, realistic versus idealistic, professional, personal, family-oriented, etc.
- The timing: short-, medium- or long-term goals.

Goals are achieved through strength and energy. Intentions create a will to live in the person who has them. Goals are related to a person's level of optimism and their level of self-esteem. It is better to set small and short-term goals than big, long-term ones.

Happiness also depends on managing emotions properly. This does not mean repressing or denying them, but identifying them and incorporating them into our lives and finding an outlet for them (expressing them). People who are capable of constructively negotiating with their emotions are happier.

Our emotional regulator works along a continuum that goes from un-controlled management at one extreme to complete control at the other. The intermediate point is emotional balance, emotional and social intelligence, which is, in general, the most desirable position and the one most closely related to happiness. People who are completely overwhelmed by their emotions are considered immature, childish, impulsive, led by their gut instinct, vulnerable, insecure and a victim of emotional contagion. Conversely, individuals who are in complete control of their emotions are considered as cold, calculating and seen to have an emotional shield.

It is not easy to control emotions. Nowhere is it taught. There are no instruction books on how to do it. The same is true of creativity. Even so, emotions are present every minute of our lives, 24 hours a day. Even as we sleep our emotions are present in our dreams.

Emotionally balanced people:

- Know how to relate to their internal world (emotional) in a specific situation. The individual is like a Roman chariot that has to be pulled by horses (emotions) in a chariot race (external reality).
- Know how to incorporate their emotions into daily life.
- Distinguish between private and public, professional and personal environments.
- Are aware of their emotions, analyse the situation and react appropriately. All this is done immediately and naturally.
- Feel their emotions and express them appropriately.

Happiness is being concerned about others, looking after them and making them happy. Very often we are too wrapped up in our own satisfaction, in our own pleasures, without realizing that the key to our happiness is in the people around us:

> Happiness is love, nothing else. A man who is capable of love is happy.
>
> (Herman Hesse)

> Only the man capable of giving can be happy.
>
> (Johann Wolfgang von Goethe)

> True happiness consists of doing right.   (Aristotle)

Happiness, then, is looking at the surrounding world from inside in a mature, realistic and enthusiastic way: 'Happiness ... consists not in seeking new landscapes, but in having new eyes' (Marcel Proust). Happiness is found within oneself and in relationships with others (partner, family, friends, colleagues, etc). It is a psychosocial balance.

In his latest book, *El cerebro infantil: la gran oportunidad*, José Antonio Marina mentions Mihaly Csikszentmihalyi, who relates happiness to the notion of *flow*. *Flow* is the experience we have when we are applying all our faculties (the feeling of complete absorption). We manage to disconnect and lose a sense of time. The philosopher Ortega y Gasset related happiness to the unification of the mental functions. I want to relate this to the synchronization between doing, feeling, communicating and thinking.

Happiness is one of the most complex concepts of the human mind. It involves all the levels that make up a person: biological, psychological, sociological, cultural and historic. To be happy, biological needs have to be fulfilled.

Different cultures and different eras may have different ideas of what happiness is. Lin Yutang, the famous Chinese language expert and writer, who was born in 1895 and died in 1976, left us his view of happiness:

> I have here the things that would make me happy. I don't want any more. I want my own room where I can work. A room neither especially clean or tidy ... but comfortable, intimate and familiar. With a smoke-filled atmosphere and the smell of old tomes and countless odours ... .

> I want decent suits that I have used for a while and a pair of old shoes. I want a shower in summer and a good log fire in winter. I want a home where I can be myself.

> I want good friends who are as familiar as life itself; friends I don't need to be polite to and who tell me all their problems, marital and otherwise; friends capable of quoting Aristotle and to recount risqué stories; friends who are spiritually rich and can speak of obscenities and philosophy with the same candour; friends who have definite passions and opinions on things, who have their beliefs and who respect mine.

> I want a good cook who knows how to make delicious dinners and an old servant who thinks I am a great man, but doesn't know in what my greatness resides.

> I want a good library, good cigars and a woman who understands me and leaves me my freedom to do my work.

> I want the freedom to be myself.

Some of the details of this extract are a product of its time, but the essence of the message is what we have been developing in this chapter: authenticity, the essence of things, spiritual richness and freedom.

I have tried in this chapter to define the key points that make up the formula for happiness. But happiness is mainly concerned with the psychological and social fields. Happiness is a feeling (psychology) and it has to be achieved in relation to others (sociology). Happiness is a state of balance, which makes the most of the singular and irreproducible being we have inside us, and where also we take into account the expectations of others and the nature of the situation.

I am particularly fond of one of Eduardo Punsent's reflections on life and death. He begins his book *Excusas para no pensar* (Excuses for not thinking) with the following dedication: 'I dedicate this book to all those who have discovered that there is life before death.' Humanity has dedicated a lot of time to pondering and investigated whether there is life after death, but it is much more important to realize that there is life before death. Live life and enjoy it!

Google the wise tells us that Matthieu Ricard is the happiest person in the world. One of the most important of Ricard's thoughts is: 'Living the experiences life offers us is mandatory, suffering because of them or enjoying them is optional.' I want to add that it is important to be honest with oneself: 'It is not good to lie to others, but the worst lies are those we tell ourselves' (Pepe Martínez).

Happiness on the biological level

One very important and basic part of happiness is having a healthy body. Being healthy means physical and psychological well-being. If we become sick this disappears: 'Health and cheerfulness mutually beget each other' (Joseph Addison).

Happiness is a good connection, integration, intercommunication and synergy between the mind and body. Looking after your body helps your emotional and psychological well-being. If we compare the human body to a car, there are three aspects that need looking after:

1 The heart and lungs (the engine). These organs are kept healthy through activities such as running, cycling and swimming.

2 The muscular system (the bodywork and chassis). A good muscle structure is achieved through physical exercise (any type of exercise).

3 The digestive system (the fuel tank). 'We are what we eat.' Our physical and psychological functioning depends on the quality of the food we eat every day.

If we look after these three aspects of our body, we will feel much better psychologically because of the connection between the mind and the body. On the physiological plane, we find that happiness is a type of physical-chemical balance. It is a balance between the nervous system and the endocrine system. It is a balance of electrical impulses (neurones), neurotransmitters (chemical substances) and hormones.

Happiness is a delicate balance between physiology, biology, psychology and the social dimension.

Happiness study at Millward Brown

At the beginning of 2011 we asked all Millward Brown employees a question about happiness. We are talking of a workforce of 3,700 employees spread over 51 countries and 77 offices worldwide.

The method used for this research was an online questionnaire. The question was: 'Describe what happiness means to you.' We received replies from 980 people. I would like to take this opportunity to thank all those who took part, and for their collaboration.

TABLE 11.1

Describe what happiness means to you	%
1 Enjoying life	12%
2 Peace, harmony and peace of mind	11.2%
3 Being comfortable with others	9.6%
4 Satisfaction	9.4%
5 Love	9.3%
6 Being at easy with oneself	7.8%
7 Not having any worries	7.2%
8 Things going the way you wanted them to go	7%
9 Having challenges and goals	6.1%
10 Family	5.6%
Base	980

I think the replies from my colleagues are pretty clear and self-explanatory. Table 11.1 shows the percentages for each response, and Figure 11.1 the words used. They show a strong correlation to everything we have seen in this chapter, and are also a good summary of the main factors influencing the achievement of happiness.

I also took the opportunity of using this research to ask three additional questions:

1 What three questions come to mind when you think of psychoanalysis treatment? (base = 1079 people).

2 The advantages of psychoanalysis (base = 596 people).

3 The disadvantages of psychoanalysis (base = 581 people).

FIGURE 11.1

The free association between psychoanalysis generated the answers shown in Table 11.2.

TABLE 11.2

What three words/ideas come to mind when you think of psychoanalysis treatment?	%
1 Freud (Sigmund Freud)	17.6%
2 Head, mind, brain	6.4%
3 Couch, sofa	6.1%
4 Psychiatry	4.4%
5 Problems	3.3%
6 Psychology	3.2%
7 Psychologist, psychoanalyst	2.8%
8 Help	2.6%
9 Talking	2.6%
10 Madness	2.5%
Base	1079

As you can see in Figure 11.2, the main associations are Freud, the mind and the couch.

FIGURE 11.2

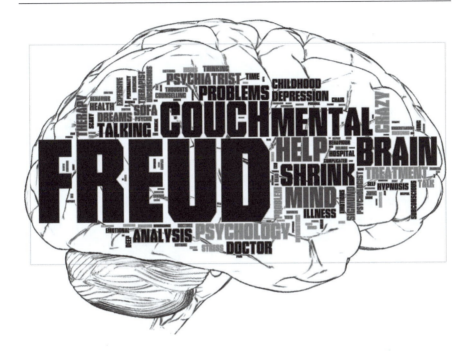

With reference to the second question (advantages of psychoanalysis), the main responses were as shown in Table 11.3.

TABLE 11.3

Advantages of psychoanalysis	%
1 To know oneself better	12.1%
2 To solve mental health problems	12%
3 To get to the root of the problem	7.7%
4 To receive help	5%
5 To dig deeper	3.7%
6 To understand problems	3%
7 To talk freely	2.9%
8 No drugs	2.3%
9 To feel better	2.2%
10 To understand behaviour	1.8%
Base	596

FIGURE 11.3

Less people replied to this question, because there is a huge lack of awareness about the advantages of psychoanalysis.

Psychoanalysis offers significant benefits. The main ones are understanding oneself better, resolving mental conflicts and reaching the root of the problem. But it also presents some disadvantages, as shown in the answers to our final question; see Table 11.4.

TABLE 11.4

Disadvantages of psychoanalysis	%
1 Think that the process is long and slow	23.2%
2 It is an expensive treatment	13.5%
3 It is invasive	3.4%
4 It is not effective	3.3%
5 It creates dependency	2.9%
6 It does not guarantee results	2.9%
7 It stigmatizes the person	2.8%
8 It is not reliable	1.9%
9 It involves suffering (brings out fears, frustation)	1.7%
10 It is rooted in the past	1.5%
Base	581

FIGURE 11.4

The highest percentage we saw in the entire research exercise (23.2 per cent), think that the process is long and slow.

Indeed it is a long, slow, expensive process. These disadvantages mean that psychoanalysis has to reposition itself within society, and it needs to design a new strategy to compete effectively with other psychotherapy methods and to be successful in attracting potential clients.

Summary of key learning points about brands

Happy brands:

- Present an original view of the world.

- Are very loyal to themselves, to their concept, and to their spirit/essence.

- Are aware and responsive to others (in this case the consumers).

- Are attractive and are an inspirational model.

- Are very coherent and consistent in what they do, say (communicate), feel and think.

- Do not baulk at difficulties or changes in the market. They are energetic, innovative and capable of reinventing themselves.

I'm off to bed!

12

> *The night suggests, it does not show. The night disquiets and surprises us with its otherness; it releases forces within us which by day are dominated by reason.*   **BRASSAI**

Time for a rest

Well, we've come a long way since the alarm clock rang, and now it is time to go to bed and close the daily cycle. Our arms are stretching, we're yawning, we're tired. Our body is asking us to rest. The body needs to repair itself after the energy it has spent and the efforts it has made during the day (the muscular system, the various bodily organs, our senses, the brain, etc).

The brain needs to go from 'on' to 'off'. Our body 'switch' needs to be turned off for this to happen. We climb into bed and gradually our mind enters into a state of somnolence: we become drowsy and then we fall asleep. The reticular formation, also known as the reticular activating system, as we saw earlier, starts to reduce the level of activation. The brain's activity level or 'arousal' level drops to a minimum. The same occurs with the rest of the body: the levels of physiological activity decrease. These hours of nightly repose are the time for all the parts of our body to recuperate and make repairs. The hypothalamus takes an active part in regulating the sleep process.

We let ourselves be overtaken by the need to rest, we prepare for bed, we get in and cover ourselves with sheets. We remember some of the things we have done during the day, or we think about the day we are going to have tomorrow, and ... voila! We are asleep. But then unexpected and strange nocturnal activities start to occur: dreams. The brain never stops, not at night, not even when you are sleeping.

There has been a great deal of study into dreams and much has been written about them. People are still trying to reveal their meaning for our bodies and minds, for our biology and psychology. The most rounded current hypothesis points to dreams having an active role in consolidating the memory processes. But since Sigmund Freud, dreams have been imbued with an importance as carriers of messages significant to the dreamer. These two hypotheses are not incompatible or interchangeable in themselves, but they could be complementary.

Dream discourse and advertising discourse

At first glance there are clear differences between a dream and an advertising spot or TV ad. However, if we look at both these forms of communication in some depth, although they appear to be very different we can find surprising points in common.

On any given day, people will remember the dream they had the night before. They probably had several dreams on that same night, but the following morning they only remember one specific dream, or part of it, which captured their attention.

A person, a dreamer, is at the same time a consumer of various products and services. The previous day, prior to the night of the dream, he, the dreamer, was watching his favourite programme; in one of the ad breaks he watched the adverts while lying on the sofa. The following day he suddenly remembered one of the 'spots' that had a particular impact on him. Of all the many adverts he saw, he remembers one in particular.

So, here we have a dream and an ad spot which, among many others, has managed to capture this person's attention; it has connected with his mind, his psychology. It has acquired a special significance for him. This did not happen by accident, rather it happened because both the dream and the advert contain messages that are of particular relevance to this person.

It is possible to establish a series of similarities between dreams and advertising spots – both are experiences of communication. The common points are as follows:

- When we remember a dream, generally we get the feeling that only a short time has passed, even when this involves a long dream. In the same way, television adverts have a short period of communicative impact (10, 20, 30, 45, 60 ... seconds).

- When we sleep we have many dreams. When we wake up we only remember a small part of them. Equally, there are a huge number of adverts on television (advertising saturation) for various products, services and brands, of which we only remember a few – the ones that have achieved most relevance in our minds.

- With both dreams and television spots, we remember those most significant for us; namely those that have connected with our unconscious, with our desires, motivations, needs, etc.

- The television advert does not have to respond to a logical structure, nor do dreams. Both are far from the rules of the conscious, rational, logical world. Both the dream and the advertising spot are governed by the laws of the unconscious and desires. They have their own licences, their own game rules, quite different to how the real world works and to everything that surrounds us. Advertising and dreams belong to the imagination, fantasy, creativity and the emotions. In a dream, for example, you may walk through the desert and find a magic lamp with a genie that appears when you rub it and grants you three wishes. In an advert, the scene is after a party; someone is cleaning a house that has been left in an absolute mess when, suddenly, a marvellous character appears (a wizard, a butler ...), emerging from a fantasy world and offering the ideal cleaning product to resolve the problem. Dreams and adverts transcend the rules of external reality and plunge us into the world of imagination and fantasy.

- Many dreams and adverts enact an idea, generally a desire or psychological need that relates directly to the dreamer or consumer. When an ad spot is created, the advertisers have to think about all the types of relationships they are going to establish with the target public (the link between the campaign and the audience), through the character or elements that are going to identify the future purchaser, and what effect the advertising formula used will produce (persuasion, credibility, stir them into buying, create resistance, etc).

- Although the auditory channel is there during dreams and adverts, the visual channel acquires a greater role. In reality, the dream, as well as the advertising spot, is the embodiment of thoughts, emotions, desires and needs, in visual images.

- Another important mechanism in the worlds of dreams and advertising is condensing ideas. Elements appear in both the dream and the advert that acquire multiple significances that need to be discovered. And they are real icons. Several possible meanings are compressed into these symbols; these need to be decoded, and may be complementary to each other. There is a polysemy of symbols.

- Both in dreams and in adverts, two levels have to be distinguished: the manifest and the latent. Things may not be what they seem, so clear differences have to be made between the empirical level (observable) and latent level (which is where the real meaning/significance is to be found).

Summary of key learning points about brands

Television spots, like the dreams we have when we sleep, share certain characteristics:

- Generally, they happen over a very short time.

- We only remember the most significant and relevant.

- They do not have to correspond to a logical structure. They have their own licence (the world of imagination, of creativity) to reach the emotional level in the viewer/dreamer.

- The visual channel plays a more prominent role than the audio.

- Both play out an idea, usually a desire or psychological need relating to the viewer/dreamer.

Summary of the brain's mental functions

13

> *Of all the tyrannies on human kind,*
> *the worst is that which persecutes the mind.* **JOHN DRYDEN**

Throughout this book we have looked at the various functions of the human mind. We have paused briefly to look at each one in depth. The remit of this book is to focus on each of the parts making up this mental or cerebral puzzle.

However, we should not lose sight of the fact that the whole is greater than the sum of its parts, and we have reached the point where we have to put it all back together. The human mind is fantastic and is a very good example of how successful teamwork can be. It is possible to explain each of the areas, but the level of interconnectivity is so great that it requires assimilation after the analysis.

As Eduardo Punset said in his book *Excusas para no pensar*, 'the brain did not just emerge spontaneously, it developed carefully over 750 million years'. Throughout this period new structures and functions were emerging and interconnections between them were being established.

Figure 13.1 shows the location of the four main mental functions:

1 Doing (motor system).
2 Feeling (emotional system).
3 Talking (communications system, language).
4 Thinking (cognitive system).

If we look more closely at each of these functions we will see a series of specific attributes, such as those shown in Figure 13.2.

FIGURE 13.1

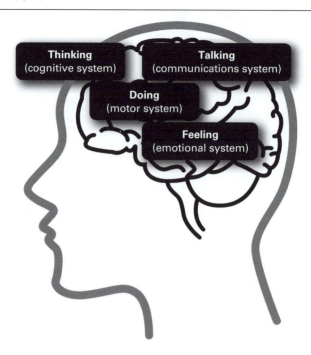

We will pause for a moment to look at this diagram. There is an area of activation and watchfulness or awareness that runs from the lower area of the brain and extends throughout the cerebral cortex. This area of the brain is also related to automatic behaviour.

Information coming from the external world reaches us through the five senses. From there it travels to the areas of perception where all sorts of messages are assimilated. The most relevant information captures the person's attention and connects with the available memory and with emotions. Later, thinking comes into play.

Within the thinking or thought area (cognitive module), which is mainly in the frontal lobes, there are several features available. These are the most advanced capabilities of our mind: they are those that have appeared most recently in the evolutionary process. And we must never forget that the human brain is continuing to evolve. We are immersed in this process. Change is always present in our lives. Nature doesn't slow down for even a fraction of a second.

The main options offered by the cognitive module are as follows:

● thought (thinking);
● planning;
● executive control;
● problem solving;

FIGURE 13.2

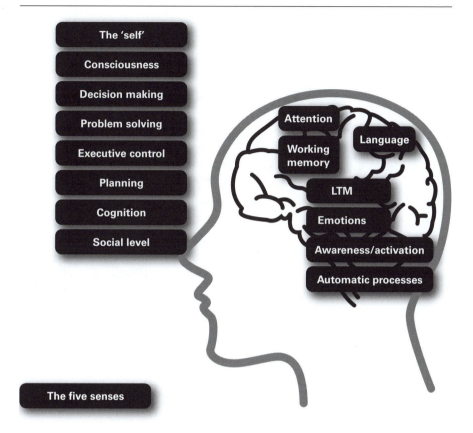

- decision making;
- consciousness;
- the 'self' that governs our life; and
- social skills.

If a person needs to communicate with other people, the language area springs into action. Words are our most powerful vehicle for communicating with others. But we must consider other forms of communication (body language, facial expressions, tone of voice, connotations, intentions, etc). In the communication process, what you say (content) is important, but even more important is the significance and intention of the message conveyed.

In Figure 13.3 I want to highlight the fact that in the lower posterior part of the brain is an area that we could call the 'maintenance area' (brain activation, automatic movements, and homeostasis if we include the hypothalamus). These functions are to be found on the ground floor of the brain's 'building'.

FIGURE 13.3

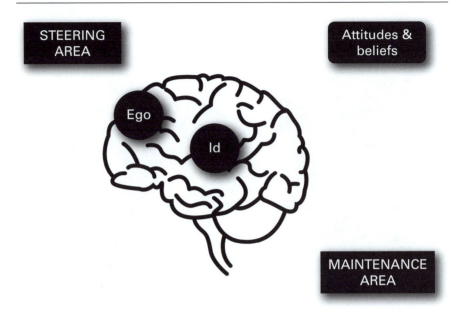

In the area diagonally opposite, in the upper anterior brain (frontal lobes) we have what we could call the 'steering area', metaphorically speaking. This is found in the upper part of the brain's 'building'.

In his second structure of the mind, Freud developed the concepts of Super-ego, Ego and Id. Obviously these are theoretical constructs, intuitive in nature, but we are going to try to relate them to the knowledge we currently have about the brain and the mind:

- We can place the Id (instincts, impulses, the primary process, the pleasure principle) in the limbic area of the brain (emotional area). It can also be related to the 'reward circuit'.

- The Ego, which tries to mediate between the Super-ego, the Id and the external reality, is in the frontal lobe, in the 'steering zone'; the Ego works on the principle of reality according to the laws of the secondary process. The reality principle and the secondary process try to free the subject from the constant need (addictive) to achieve immediate pleasure. They show how to postpone the reward. These psychological concepts are very similar to a financial concept that is much celebrated at the moment: ROI or 'return on investment'.

- The Super-ego is the voice of your conscience; it is about standards and rules to be complied with. It represents duty. It is a mental construct that asks us to account for ourselves, that pushes us to do good, to take responsibility. As Freud would say, it urges us to love and to work. Could we also relate the Super ego with prefrontal lobe activity? The future will give us the answer.

I placed the words 'attitudes and beliefs' in the upper right part of Figure 13.3. Attitudes and beliefs are not located in a specific part of the brain or mind. They emerge from a combination of various cognitive, emotional and experiential (memory) areas. Our attitudes towards others, to the world around us, to life and to ourselves, have been taking shape since we were very young. Attitude is a thought and feelings-based construct, that makes us react in a specific way towards others and towards the external reality.

I am saying this because in market research it is very important to accurately identify consumers' attitudes and beliefs, because these will give us the most incisive insights for designing a good brand strategy, to communicate and to have an effective media plan.

Summary of key learning points about brands

The goal of any brand is:

- To enter through the five senses.

- To capture the consumers' attention.

- To connect with their needs, values and desires.

- To create an emotional link (feeling, the affective system).

- To leave a long-term imprint in their memory.

- To positively influence the decision-making process (doing, the instant of purchase for the product, or signing a contract for a service).

- To create a good brand experience (remember Damasio's somatic-marker concept).

- To maintain the item as 'front of mind' within its category.

- To create a powerful and positive 'word of mouth' (talking, the language system). Recommendations from consumers have become as important, arguably more important, than recommendations from manufacturers or opinion leaders.

- To encourage repeat purchases and brand loyalty.

Brands, communications and the mind

14

"Products are made in the factory, but brands are created in the mind. **WALTER LANDOR**

The brand's function

There are people even today who confuse a brand with its logo, reducing the brand to its signature. There are also those who view a brand as something that is merely cosmetic, as if the brand name were a type of 'make-up' applied to the product or the service, but a brand is not a decorative element.

The brand name is a very profound concept. It is a promise of a unique value. And this promise has to be fulfilled with an experience that is gratifying to the body and/or mind of the consumer. A gratifying experience is key. The external reality (a product's characteristics or the brand's attributes) are determined by the internal reality (the psychological dimension, the person's experience).

The brand has to be original. The worst thing that can happen to a brand is for it to be a copy of another, a replica, a 'me too'. Imitations directly attack the concept of the brand itself and are against its very essence.

Brands exist thanks to the fact that the brain and mind are capable of working with intangibles. A brand is an attractive and aspirational world for consumers. A brand has to attract people like a magnet. It has to create interest. Afterwards, there must be consumer satisfaction to achieve loyalty (repeat purchase).

A brand is a living reality. It has to be dynamic. It has to be active. It has to be present in the life and mind of consumers. It has to stimulate their brain. It has to generate emotions and make them excited. It has to communicate passion and enthusiasm.

A brand has to be genuine, faithful to its principles and values. In this sense it has to behave and communicate in a consistent way. It will change, surprise, innovate ... but in a way that is consistent with the brand's essence. Brands have a certain margin for manoeuvre, but they cannot move away from their reason for being. They cannot echo what the famous actor and comic wit, Groucho Marx said: 'Those are my principles, and if you don't like them ... well, I have others.'

These days, mature markets are saturated and brands have to be very relevant, creative, effective and efficient. It has been observed that it costs more (energy, money) to capture the attention of a new mind (potential consumer) than to retain the loyalty of a current consumer, offering them better and new brand experiences.

Five different aspects of a brand should be distinguished:

1 its values;

2 its products or services;

3 its communications;

4 the scenarios it develops (media plan and 'touch points') – contrary to what many think, creativity and the ability to achieve a significant impact can be more important than the size of the budget; and

5 the most important: the consumer (the target audience).

New challenges for brands

The market always presents new challenges. This may involve opening up markets in emerging countries where brands have to adapt to very different cultures and where they have to connect with very different consumers.

For mature markets, the biggest problem is saturation and the difficulties differentiation presents. Since most brands carry out their own market research, they really understand consumers' tastes and they adapt to them as closely as possible. This is why it is so important to achieve those small differences between products, which are perceived as enormous added value in the mind.

In mature markets, brands are having to adapt when trying to reach the industrial, business to business (B2B) sector. Here, unlike fast moving consumer goods (FMCG), the products and services are less attractive, less glamorous and offer fewer opportunities to resort to the 'licence' offered by imagination and creativity. Brands also offer huge possibilities when it comes to differentiating between, and being attractive to, different geographical locations. Brands are heading towards the concept of territorial brands: country brands, regional brands, city brands (city marketing), town brands, etc. By the same token the idea of branding is reaching official bodies, associations, museums, etc. It is also reaching out to the small and medium sized business (SME) sector: shops/stores, self-employed people, and even personal branding. The more saturated the world market becomes, the greater the need for differentiation.

The keys to brand success

Our colleagues at Millward Brown Optimor carry out an annual survey to identify the 100 most valuable global brands; they have done so every year from 2005 onwards. In 2005 and 2006 the top brand was Microsoft. In 2007, 2008 and 2009 the top brand was Google. We will see below that there has been a change in the ranking: in 2010 Google moved into second place. I won't reveal who the new leader is, because I am trying to create a little intrigue and pique your curiosity.

Google is a brand that is about the same age as my daughter Patricia, who is now a teenager. In its relatively short life it has become the most powerful brand in the world. But why has Google been the leading brand for three years? Because it fulfils five key requirements or conditions:

1 It is original and unique: when it first started there was no other brand providing such a complete service.

2 It is attractive: when we need any type of information quickly, we think of clicking on this search engine. Google connects really well with consumers' needs. Brands always have to be very alert to, and very aware of the desires, values, lifestyles, trends, etc of their consumers. Coca-Cola, Nivea and Danone all do this. This is why, despite being brands with a long history, they are still in very good shape. When a brand slips from the consumer's mind, it starts to age; the wrinkles start to appear. Coca-Cola is very close to the tastes of new generations. Nivea started as a blue box containing cream, and now it has a very modern, and very full, line of products, capable of satisfying quite diverse audiences. The same is true of Danone, which began as a simple yoghurt in a glass jar, and now it has a range of dairy-based products that help maintain consumers' health (Activia, Actimel, Danacol, Densia, etc).

3 Google is, paradoxically, very complicated (it holds everything) and very simple (always to hand) at the same time: it is really easy to use and anyone can access Google to search for the information they need. There are products and services on the market that only people with advanced technical knowledge can use; this is not the case with Google because it works in a way that is very similar to the human mind. It is a brand that 'performs' very empathetically.

4 It is practical: the service this brand offers is very useful. It has a multitude of functions. It is a brand that constantly helps you.

5 And, finally the price is reasonable: it is good value for money. The equilibrium between what you get from the brand and what you pay for it is balanced. You have to make a very clear distinction between cost and value. The cost of a product or service is what you have to pay for it, its price. But its value is something much more important, because it refers to what the consumer is prepared to pay for that article. The value of a product is linked to what it means to the consumer.

Figure 14.1 shows the five requirements a brand has to fulfil to be successful.

FIGURE 14.1

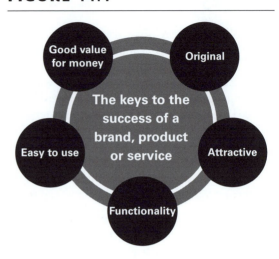

Whenever we are about to launch a new brand, a new product or service onto the market, we always test it …we have to take account of the response to these five characteristics. This template is a good indicator of the level of success it will have on the market. If it really fulfils each and every one of the requirements, we can think in terms of good business. But if it does not, it would be advisable to think again and start improving on the idea.

Brand leaders

The new global brand leader in 2010

As I said previously, Millward Brown Optimor have carried out a study into the 100 most powerful global brands for a number of years; the research covering 2010 was published in May 2011. It is the only ranking that combines quantitative market research with the financial results for the brands, showing the brands' value in US dollars. Over 2 million interviews were carried out in 30 countries, in 13 sectors:

Clothing	Beer
Automobiles	Fast food
Financial entities	Insurance
Luxury goods	Petrol and gas
Personal care	Distribution
Soft drinks	Technology
Telecommunications companies	

Finally, the time has come to reveal the secret: in 2010 Apple became the world's most valuable brand, beating Google. Apple responds very closely to the keys for a successful brand:

- Originality.
- Attractiveness: fascinating.
- Functionality.
- Ease of use: it is a brand that empathizes strongly with the consumer. Its technology and functions adapt very well to the needs of the human mind.
- Reasonable price. Here we mean value for money; we recognize that the price is not one of the main advantages of Apple.
- In return, it offers innovation and design, which helps to offset and compensate for the effect of the price.

It is clear that everyone employed at Apple has a strong commitment to the brand and it is the highest priority for all of them.

The 10 most powerful brands in the world in 2010

Table 14.1 lists the world's 10 leading brands.

TABLE 14.1 Top 10 global brands

Rank	Brand	Brand value ($m)
1	Apple	153,285
2	Google	111,498
3	IBM	100,849
4	McDonald's	81,016
5	Microsoft	78,243
6	Coca-Cola	73,752
7	AT&T	69,916
8	Marlboro	67,522
9	China Mobile	57,326
10	General Electric (GE)	50,318

MillwardBrown
Optimor

Seven of the 10 leading brands are in the technology and telecommunications sector: Apple, Google, IBM, Microsoft, AT&T, China Mobile and General Electric (GE). Technology has become the new science, magic, art and religion. For some consumers it is like an addiction. Technology generates strong emotions in people: surprise, fascination, confidence in oneself, omnipotence ... even anger when things don't work properly.

Technology is the natural means of communication for the new generation. My son David is about to turn 18. He is a completely different person in face-to-face relationships compared to relationships he has through his BlackBerry. While in direct relationships things are not easy (he is at a difficult age), through BlackBerry messages he shows himself to be a much nicer person (he sends me messages, he tells me things, we have fun, very often he writes 'ha, ha, ha', he uses smiley faces ...). It is as if I have twin sons: the real relationship David, and the virtual relationship David.

I mentioned this during a talk I was giving at a conference about technology recently. In the coffee break, one of the attendees came up to me and told me that the same happened to him with his three sons. He played on the PlayStation and everything is fun, laughter and togetherness. Immediately afterwards they sit down to dinner and communication shuts down.

My daughter Patricia has just turned 15. I was really surprised that on her birthday the present she was most delighted with was a BlackBerry (well, and some shoes with very high heels). In a very short time this brand has expanded its appeal to an audience made up of young people and teenagers. Javito, the son of a friend of mine, who is only 12, already has a BlackBerry.

When group discussions (qualitative research) involving teenagers are organized, they become difficult to moderate because the participants find the surroundings too artificial and they have difficulty in using their communications systems. However, these same people will actively participate in the group dynamic if this is done virtually (online).

We must always look for the research method that is the most natural and least invasive for each target audience. This is the best way to obtain better quality information.

The 10 brands with most growth during 2010

The ten brands that experienced the most growth in 2010 are shown in Table 14.2.

Facebook topped the list. With a 246 per cent rise in brand value, Facebook entered the BrandZ Top 100 for the first time at number 35. The Top 20 Risers included online retailer Amazon and four other technology brands – Apple and Baidu along with Siemens and Cannon, which benefited from a resurgence in B2B demand. Visionary, entrepreneurial leadership also contributed to growth in value, especially for Facebook, Apple, Amazon and Starbucks.

TABLE 14.2 10 top risers in 2010

Rank	Brand	Growth
1	Facebook	246%
2	Baidu	141%
3	Wells Fargo	97%
4	Burberry	86%
5	Apple	84%
6	Skol	68%
7	Pizza Hut	58%
8	GEICO	53%
9	Standard Chartered Bank	45%
10	Hermès	41%

MillwardBrown
Optimor

With almost 600 million members worldwide, Facebook was anointed 'The Social Network' by the film of the same name about the firm's founding in 2004 by Mark Zuckerberg. Ironically, the film's release coincided with Facebook's rapid evolution into a powerful commercial platform exploring ways to monetize its social reach by connecting shoppers, retailers and brand marketers.

Apple rose to the number 1 position in the BrandZ Top 100 most valuable global brands. It earned an 84 per cent increase in brand value with successful iterations of existing products like the iPhone, creation of the tablet category with iPad, and anticipation of a broadened strategy making the brand a trifecta of cloud computing, software, and innovative, well-designed devices.

The Chinese search engine Baidu ranked 29 in the BrandZ Top 100, up from 75 in 2009 on a sharp 141 per cent rise in brand value. As more of China's 1.3 billion citizens used the internet, they turned to Baidu because the brand has really understood the nuances of China's diverse cultures and languages.

Illustrating how dramatically shopping has changed, Amazon surpassed Walmart as the most valuable retail brand. The company has continued to add categories each year, even food, to drive traffic. Since founding the company in 1995, Jeff Bezos has worked to perfect its unparalleled selection, peer reviews and a delivery scheme that builds loyalty.

Starbucks' 40 per cent rise in brand value demonstrated the success of the brand revitalization initiatives implemented recently by Howard Schultz when he returned as CEO. He closed underperforming sites and improved the coffeehouse experience while extending the brand into instant coffee and preparing it for aggressive international and multi-channel growth in grocery as well as fast food.

The housing recovery drove IKEA's 28 per cent growth. The sector's strength also helped brands in fast food, insurance and luxury goods. While the brand value of the luxury sector still lagged its pre-recession level, customers came back, as evinced by Burberry's 86 per cent increase and the brand appreciation of Cartier, Estée Lauder and Hermès.

The market dynamism that boosted China's Baidu also pushed up the brand values of Skol, Brazil's largest beer brand, by 68 per cent, and Petrobras, the country's oil and gas giant, which improved 39 per cent. The 58 per cent rise in the brand value of Pizza Hut was in part driven by its performance in China. Standard Chartered Bank of the UK, up 45 per cent, also benefited from global business.

All sectors grew in brand value in 2010

Each of the 12 product sectors measured in the BrandZ Top 100 ranking appreciated in overall brand value in 2010. Table 14.3 shows the growth achieved for each of these sectors during 2010.

The performance dramatically differed from results a year earlier, when just four sectors improved only moderately in brand value. It signalled a shift in the global economy from recovery to growth. It also demonstrated the resilience of brands. Brand value in many sectors not only appreciated year-on-year, but also exceeded pre-recession levels. Fast food, which climbed a substantial 22 per cent in 2010 alone, was up 42 per cent when compared with 2008.

Technology improved too: 18 per cent year-on-year compared with 32 per cent over the three-year period. The story was similar for beer, which grew 7 per cent in 2010 but 32 per cent since the recession. Soft drinks grew 5 per cent in 2010 and 26 per cent since 2008.

Categories hardest hit during the recession posted gains in brand value in 2010, but the values remain below pre-recession levels. Luxury returned robustly but, with 19 per cent increase in brand value, the category remained 13 per cent lower than its 2008 level.

The car sector grew by 7 per cent in 2010 on the rebound of the resilient Toyota brand, strong performances by Ford, GM and other major car makers, and the appetite for 'status' cars in China and other fast-growing markets. Brand value for the car sector as a whole, however, remained 27 per cent below its 2008 level.

TABLE 14.3 All sectors grew in brand value in 2010

Rank	Sector	Growth (2010 versus 2009)
1	Insurance	137%
2	Fast-food	22%
3	Luxury	19%
4	Technology	18%
5	Apparel	10%
6	Financial institutions	9%
7	Beer	7%
8	Cars	7%
9	Soft drinks	5%
10	Personal care	3%
11	Retail	2%
12	Oil & gas	1%

 MillwardBrown
Optimor

While apparel, personal care, oil and gas, retail and financial institutions moved at slower rates, they all moved up. The dramatic year-on-year rise for the insurance sector was down to the inclusion of three large, fast-growing Chinese brands: China Life, Ping An and China Pacific.

Building brands

Brands and the cinema

Many technology-related brands (designed for face-to-face or virtual relationships) are constantly involved in research in order to conquer the hearts (emotions) and pockets of consumers. I'll give you some examples:

- Apple (number 1).
- Google (number 2).
- BlackBerry (number 25).
- Facebook (number 35).

These are just a few of the many brands immersed in the technology battle to conquer the minds of consumers in the real or digital worlds, or even both.

It is interesting to see how the brands Apple and Google communicate. They appear in many cinema films. Virtually every time an actor picks up a computer, we can see the bitten apple on its very modern exterior design. And when you see the inside, the screen, then it is Google's turn. This is how the two most powerful brands on the planet convey their leadership.

The film 'Buried' shows a young man who wakes up buried in a wooden coffin, who uses his BlackBerry to get help. It is a film specially designed for this brand. (I won't tell you the ending just in case you haven't seen the film but want to.) In the case of Facebook the communication is even more brazen. The film 'The Social Network' recreates all the conflicts and successes of the birth, development and success of this brand.

The world's most valuable brands try to use product placement to be seen (in a natural way) in new films. It is a way of keeping themselves alive in consumers' minds.

Recipes for building strong, healthy brands

I have taken the following conclusions from the Millward Brown Optimor survey on the 100 most valuable global brands. The strongest brands succeeded in the following ways:

- Connecting with consumers' minds:
  - Listening closely to them.
  - Talking to them.
  - Anticipating change.
  - Understanding change.
  - Acting as quickly as possible (faster than their competitors), offering functions, etc that are relevant to consumers (it is about achieving a significant impact).
- Looking after the product to the greatest extent possible:
  - Innovating (easy to say, difficult to achieve).
  - Committing themselves to originality (if it is different it captures the mind's attention).
  - Creating a good brand experience (having satisfied customers).
  - Fulfilling the brand's promise (the feeling of trust and credibility).
  - Offering value at an affordable price (the right price).

- Communicating well:
  - Being clear and having an impact (because this makes messages easier to understand and to remember).
  - Openness and transparency (because this generates credibility).
  - Conveying confidence.
  - Being honest.
  - Measuring communication activities in the real and the digital world (social media).
- And, finally, protecting the brand:
  - Differentiated personality.
  - Being consistent with the brand's essence and strategy, but at the same time having a clear margin for manoeuvre (flexibility).
  - Breaking the rules in the present to create a future.
  - Corporate social responsibility (CSR): a sincere commitment, relevant to the consumer and coherent with the essence of the brand.

The Nigel Hollis and Gordon Pincott model

It is worthwhile pausing for a moment to look at the 'Value Drivers Model' created by my colleagues Nigel Hollis and Gordon Pincott. Nigel and Gordon have spent a major part of their professional careers on brands and their corresponding communications, and have constructed models to explain a brand's level of success. Their focus will help us understand the key points to a brand's success. Here is what they have to say.

The 'Value Drivers Model', shown in Figure 14.2, has been developed as a framework to help clients identify how best to grow the value of their brand.

The model is the result of extensive analysis of our brand equity database and a re-evaluation of earlier models in the light of new evidence. The model has been discussed with a number of clients worldwide to assess how well it matches up to real-life marketing challenges. This has convinced us that the 'Value Drivers Model' is generally applicable and provides a good road map for how businesses can increase the financial return from their brands.

The model consists of two basic steps: 1) Define: What does the brand offer that is meaningfully different from other brands in the category? 2) Amplify: How best can that difference be amplified across the brand experience? A clear definition of what makes the brand meaningfully different to its customers is an essential prerequisite before deciding how to amplify it.

The model addresses two key issues facing brand marketing today. The first of these is that there are many more possibilities of taking a brand to market and many more channels of communication to be harnessed. The consequence of this growing complexity is that businesses are often much more focused on the amplification without having clearly defined what it is that needs to be amplified. It is also true in developing markets that gaining

FIGURE 14.2 Value Drivers Model (Nigel Hollis and Gordon Pincott, (*How brands drive value growth*)

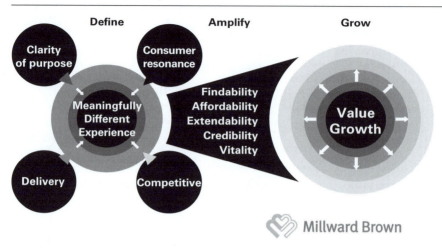

distribution and finding the right price point become obsessions for businesses, often to the exclusion of thinking through why people buy the brand and how that can be focused and enhanced.

Secondly we find that with so many amplification opportunities available to them, businesses are not necessarily thinking through all of the possible ways in which they can reach out to their customers and can become overly focused on the latest 'hot' marketing techniques.

Define

We can see the different variables the model takes into account in the first stage (defining a meaningfully different experience):

- clarity of purpose;
- delivery;
- consumer resonance;
- competitive offer.

Why is 'a meaningfully different experience' important? People choose brands they find to be meaningfully different, a perception that creates a desire to buy the brand. If the brand seems positively different it will be able to command a price premium. If the difference makes the brand seem great value then it will command a higher volume of sales.

It is the role of marketing to shape the interface between consumer perception and reality to grow the financial value of the brand. To do so, four things must coincide. The first two, purpose and delivery, are under the brand owner's direct control. The second pair, consumer resonance and competitive offer, are external factors against which the brand offer is judged.

1. Clarity of purpose

Why does the brand exist? Purpose refers to the difference a brand intends to make in people's lives. To be successful a brand must resolve a consumer need, want or desire. The need may be functional, emotional, aspirational or, increasingly, societal.

The organization needs to be aligned around a clear understanding of the brand's purpose. This means that it will speak with one voice and be single-minded in its focus. Increasingly embedded in this purpose is a social aspiration, sometimes expressed as being the pursuit of a brand ideal that goes beyond the functional delivery of the product.

The heritage of the brand and its story are elements that inform the purpose of a brand. The greater alignment of an organization behind a clearly expressed purpose, the greater chance there will be of having a successful brand. Brands with an inspirational leader often naturally have this focus because in that person they have a brand artist who is passionately concerned about the brand as well as being in a position of overall authority.

2. Delivery

Having a clear purpose for the brand is important but the brand must then live up to its purpose. Ideally a brand should deliver an outstanding experience. This would include all the elements of functional branding that encompass the product, all the details of the packaging, the physical communication to the customer (eg invoices, instruction booklets).

Outstanding design can add an aesthetic power to this functionality. For service businesses the human delivery of the purpose is at the heart of the brand delivery, but it would also include the wider experience of the brand of the kind delivered through retail outlets, car dealerships, transactional websites and so on. A shared culture will need to ensure consistent service delivery.

3. Consumer resonance

For the brand's offer to be meaningful and valuable it must resonate with the target consumer. The brand must fill an unmet customer need or fill a current need better than existing alternatives and create a positive emotional response because of the personal relevance it has.

The tighter the definition of the audience the easier it will be to create consumer resonance, but this could artificially constrain the brand's volume sales potential. The art of marketing is to make the brand as relevant as possible to as many people as possible without losing clarity about what the brand stands for.

4. Competitive offer

Whether a brand offers something different can only be defined by the competitive context.

Differentiation is most potent when it is intrinsic, that is, based on relevant, tangible and positive advantages that can be experienced through the senses. Intrinsic differentiation can be experienced in the look, feel, sound, smell, or taste of a product. However, differentiation can also be extrinsic, that is, not based on physical attributes and ingredients. Distinctive communication, provenance, a track record of innovation, or, increasingly, social and environmental responsibility can all form the basis of perceived differentiation.

The degree of differentiation required for a brand to grow and prosper will depend on the nature of the brand and category. The key question to ask is whether your brand is different enough within its competitive context. The competitive context is not controlled by the brand but is a significant factor in its success. Brands that want to continue to grow need to respond effectively to the emergence of new competitive offers. One of the reasons that brands stagnate or decline is that they have lost their original meaningful differentiation – not because of anything they have done but because of the changing landscape in which they operate.

Meaningfully different experience

The combination of the four areas will determine whether a brand is meaningfully different and how strongly the brand experience reflects that difference. The more powerful the experience the more effective all the means of amplification will be.

Amplify

Now we will look at the variables involved in the second stage (the phenomena of brand extension):

1 findability;
2 affordability;
3 extendability;
4 credibility; and
5 vitality.

1. Findability

Physical availability is vital to the success of a brand. Without adequate distribution a new brand introduction will fail and an established brand will fail to maximize its potential. Is the brand available at the place and time where people want to encounter it and purchase it? Have all the possible places been explored and thought through?

Findability also requires the brand be easily identified at the point of purchase. Is the brand identity familiar and easily recognized?

2. Affordability

The interaction of price and meaningful difference is a major consideration in growing value. One of the most important roles marketing can play is to frame price perceptions to best advantage.

Given the audience you are hoping to gain your customers from, does the brand have the right price point? Are there ways of making the product more accessible to more people in this audience (eg through pack sizing)? Are there different versions of the brand that are still based on the meaningful difference but are justifiably different so that they can sensibly appeal to different consumer segments? Are there financial mechanisms (eg hire purchase) that would allow people into the market who might struggle to access the brand? Are there new ways in which you can frame people's understanding of the brand's value and better justify a price premium? This might not just be about driving prices or price points down. If the experience is very powerful, can you raise the price to maximize the value created by the power of the brand?

3. Extendability

A major way of growing brand value is by extending a brand that has been successful in one country into other countries. It may also be possible to extend a brand from its existing categories into other categories using the power of the brand name to open up new market opportunities.

4. Credibility

It is important that the brand aligns with the experience it offers to its customers. The brand's meaningful difference can be refreshed and enhanced through innovation within the core of the product, launching new lines that benefit from, and feed back into, the meaningful difference. There will be aspects of marketing that can also increase credibility (eg affiliation with another property such as a charity, a sports star, an event).

5. Vitality

It is crucial that a brand is seen to be alive and active, a brand that is both popular and contemporary. Communication activities of all kinds involving both controlled communications and social communications build the vitality of the brand, making it visible and current. They also encourage the 'talkability' of the brand.

Communities are powerful in connecting consumers to one another. All of this activity should be driven by the meaningful difference of the brand, which means that the selection of channels and the creative content must be aligned with and driven by the meaningful experience. Vitality will also be enhanced by a brand looking and feeling fresh, which implies innovation in product packaging, logo as well as communication, but without losing clarity and identity.

The digital revolution

Shoppers and brands share the power in the new commercial democracy. The numbers tell the story. Apple is the world's most valuable brand, followed by Google. Facebook, just seven years old, appears in the BrandZ Top 100 most valuable global brands for the first time, at number 35.

While the meteoric rise of these technology brands is compelling, equally important is their impact on other sectors, as brands in every product segment respond to the fast-changing world of digitized and disintermediated information. Brands reach customers on brand and retailer websites, on Google and other search engines and on mobile apps that rewarded shoppers for interacting with brands. Some brands led the way; others attempted to catch up. Few ignored the tide. As recent events in the Middle East demonstrate, digitally connected people wield enormous power to express their desires and influence each other and events. The analogy to brands is imperfect, but both involve respect and reciprocal trust.

In these digitally enabled relationships, the role of marketer as brand builder, selling products to the public, is supplanted by the role of marketer as brand enabler, engaging the public's help to improve products and raise customer satisfaction.

In a digital creation story, the universe isn't completed on the sixth day. It's a work in progress, a partnership aimed at perpetual renewal and relevance. One element remains the same, however – the desire for an apple.

Let's talk about collaboration and co-creation. At the beginning of 2010, few people fretted that their lives were poorer due to the lack of a digital gadget smaller than their laptop but larger than their mobile phone. By the end of 2010, however, around 18 million of us owned iPads or other tablets.

Apple understood that its customers wanted access to data and images anywhere, anytime, in easy-to-view definition with an easy-to-use touch interface. In a span of a few months, the brand met these needs with the iPad and iPhone 4. Apple trusted that its customers would discover uses for these products that would help organize, simplify or complicate, but mostly improve their lives. This co-creation approach resulted in roughly 350,000 Apple applications and it added value to the product and the brand. Thousands more Android applications were created.

In a similar co-creation, brands improved products and marketing based on comments from customers in conversations on social networking sites. Co-creation was also the basis of collective shopping sites such as Groupon, which help merchants and brands increase sales and shoppers increase savings. Digital enables strangers to connect around something they share in common – the desire for a bargain.

Let's move on now to the shift in how we view customers. When brands enjoyed sovereign control over the dissemination of information about themselves, marketers could choose a demographic – for example, 18 to 24-year-old women – and design an attention-grabbing, persuasive 30-second TV commercial. That's changed. Some of our interests cut across the traditional demographic categories, often making our age and gender designations less relevant than whether it's Monday morning or Saturday night and whether we're focused on planning for the week or for our next vacation.

Brand success requires recognizing this change and allowing customers to self-identify, form groups, and access utilities and dynamic, well-built libraries of information. Last year, Pampers, number 34 in brand value, launched an iPad app called 'Welcome Baby'. It illustrated the development of a foetus in the womb and helped expectant parents understand and track the stages of pregnancy.

This kind of information is the currency of the digital democracy. It changes the brand-customer interaction from a series of isolated transactions into an ongoing relationship that becomes deeper and more interconnected. With each encounter, the customer gains more knowledge about the brand and brand-related topics and the brand learns more about the customer.

Sustaining these relationships depends on transparency and trust from both sides, brand and customer. Both sides lose if the relationship deteriorates because brands collect information using stealth tactics or customers respond with a subterfuge of false information.

The language of love in social media: new rules for brand engagement

Social media is everywhere. Pick up almost any newspaper or magazine and you will find a story referencing social media. The person sitting next to you on the bus or train or plane is probably checking his or her wall on Facebook for the latest posts or tweeting about some interesting event via his or her mobile phone. Even at work, you may catch a glimpse of someone posting a status update, blogging about some topic of interest, or watching an entertaining video on YouTube. There is so much happening in social media that we now have a whole industry of experts whose job it is to follow this movement and make sense of it for those few of us left who haven't joined the party and/or for marketers who want to cash in on it.

In just the last few years, it is quite evident that social media has turned from an interesting curiosity into a full-blown phenomenon. Watching social media go mainstream has made us at Firefly Millward Brown want – and need – to know more. In addition, we have seen the need to help our clients figure out what social media is all about, what it means for them, and how it will impact their marketing strategies. Some of the areas we wanted to explore are:

- How are brands viewed in social media and how effectively are they shaping consumer perceptions and behaviour?
- What are consumers' general attitudes and behaviours regarding social media?
- How much do attitudes and behaviours vary by country and culture – and does social media really transcend borders?
- And finally, what is the potential for using social media as a recruiting and research tool in future qualitative projects?

I would like to thank Cécile Conaré for conducting and coordinating this research. Let's start with the design of this survey carried out by the international Firefly Millward Brown team in 2010. We began with the premise that by using the medium to research the medium, we would get a more realistic portrait of users and their attitudes and behaviours. This study was an iterative, multi-phase project involving research in 15 countries:

Australia	Brazil	China
Colombia	Czech Republic	India
Indonesia	The Netherlands	Singapore
South Africa	Spain	Thailand
United Kingdom	United States	Vietnam

In each market, research was conducted among a sample of people ranging in age from 18 to 50, who represented a mix of demographics (gender, marital status, education, income and ethnicity). We further segmented individual respondents into two groups: 'moderates' (lighter users of social media) and 'mavens' (heavier, savvier users of social media). Respondents were recruited using traditional database recruiting as well as online through message boards on sites such as Facebook, Twitter and Craigslist. Using social media increased the speed of recruiting and built a stronger base of qualified respondents.

The project was divided into four phases:

1 *Client grounding.* We began by interviewing a number of client companies about their perceptions of social media and the impact it has had on their businesses. Across all markets, we interviewed more than 25 company representatives via telephone.

2 *Social media diaries.* Phase 2 involved the creation of social media diaries (on Blogger.com) to better understand consumers' attitudes and behaviours regarding social media as well as perceptions of brands and the impact of social media on purchase decisions. This phase consisted of a sample of approximately 24 respondents in each market, with a relatively even split between moderate and maven user groups.

3 *Social media drivers and deep dive.* We created a Facebook group in each market for the 24 respondents recruited in Phase 2 (except in China where we used RenRen, given the government controls on

Facebook). Using this approach, we were able to question respondents on various topics and dig a bit deeper using a more natural tool (Facebook groups being a somewhat familiar construct for our recruits).

4 *Cross-cultural insight session.* Finally, we selected two or three of the most engaged respondents from the previous two phases of research in each market. We brought this multinational group of 20-plus respondents together to participate in an IdeaBlog™ session – a proprietary Firefly Millward Brown research tool that is part blog and part online community.

Over the course of four days we posted topics and polls for our respondents to comment on and discuss. We supplemented the IdeaBlog with web-enabled 'video' interviews, which allowed us to put a face on our online respondents while exploring some unique individual topics related to social media.

We realized that there was a different consumer-brand dynamic in social media. Companies around the world clearly recognize the potential and importance of social media; the question is: how are they doing so far? When we talked to some of our client companies in the initial phase of research, most acknowledged that they have yet to figure out social media. Many are clearly struggling in the space. Why?

First, most companies have not built it into their organizational structure. They have few, if any, staff dedicated to the function. They are not even sure who in the company should take responsibility for it. Second, they are reluctant to hand over control of their brands to the consumer. As one of our packaged goods clients told us, 'Giving up control scares us. We know that social media works best when things are wildly out of control and that is the opposite of what we have traditionally been used to. We've controlled the message – the conversation.' Third, many companies perceive that they lack relevant content that could be shared in social media with consumers. Finally, they don't know enough about the space to see just how radically the landscape has shifted. Many of these companies lack even a basic understanding of social media – the platforms, the users and the rules of engagement that have quickly been established.

As a result, most marketers have taken one of two paths with regard to social media: they haven't ventured in yet or they are jumping in because they feel they 'have to be there' without really knowing what they should be doing. Both of these approaches usually produce negative results. Approach 1 – staying away – severely limits the brand's ability to stay current and relevant while making it that much harder to learn the nuances of the medium. Approach 2 – jumping in without thinking – can create huge problems if the brand takes a traditional marketing approach, as most brands often do. Indeed, many brands seem to be defaulting to old axioms like 'reach and frequency' when marketing their products and services in social media. That kind of approach is destined for failure. A critical issue for most brands is that they are not aware of (or are not following) the 'rules' that govern social media. Ultimately, the consumer expects brands to act more like friends than corporations:

> The best relationship I can have with a brand would be the same that I have with any other person through Facebook, as a friend, that I can see the updates and make a comment or not, to know that I can ask questions and comment on a subject I saw in other means of communication, as well as stop being its friend if it starts getting too boring, etc. The companies should not annoy us with ads that give us the impression that all they want is to push something on you.

They don't want to be 'sold' in the traditional sense – they'd prefer to be wooed or courted as in 'real life' by someone who is genuinely interested in them and wants to build a real relationship. As a respondent in Brazil stated:

> Starting on social networks is like starting a marriage. You have to work hard to be your best, you have to put some effort into it, contribute, surrender yourself, give up a lot of things and always care about innovating and doing something different to avoid boredom. It's the same thing with social networks – after you're in, you need to have time and patience to publish cool stuff, whether it's videos, photos or just regular posts. It's hard work to commit to this new order.

More than anything, consumers want brands to remember that social media is a community, not a marketplace.

There are deep emotional drivers behind social media's appeal. The last few years have seen explosive growth in social media. The latest statistics show that Facebook has over 500 million active users (Facebook.com/statistics/2010). A key question is why. Why have so many of us embraced it? What is it about social media that really draws us to it? What deep-seated needs and desires does it fulfil?

First, it's about connectedness and belonging. Second, it's about entertainment and, ultimately, escapism. Third, it's about control – the engine that really drives social media and is its unique appeal. The specific activities at the core of social networking have emotional meaning as well. Every post represents a need to be recognized and acknowledged by those around us. Every comment left or shared is really just our way of seeking validation.

These underlying emotional factors – sense of control, belonging, escapism, validation and recognition – all shape how consumers react to brands in social media – and offer guidance to brands as they attempt to engage consumers more effectively.

Social media impacts our attitudes and behaviour

Everyone seems to be an extrovert now – seeking more and more 'friends' or connections and willing to share just about anything and everything with those in their social networks. Examples abound where people share everything, from serious illnesses to what they ate for breakfast, even to crimes they may have committed. (During the course of this research study, respondents freely divulged details about their children, lack of employment and other personal hardships, as if they were in therapy.)

All this has erased any notion of what used to be called 'over-sharing' or 'too much information'. There is no such thing anymore. Paradoxically, people are becoming more private with their personal data. Information such as one's date of birth, identification or National Insurance number, even physical address, is closely guarded. There are indications that people worry they might be exploited either in the real world or by marketers if they give access to this personal information.

Finally, the quality of our relationships also seems to have been negatively impacted with the growth of social media. In a world of social media, emphasis is placed on quantity over quality. More is made of the numbers – how many friends or followers you have – than depth and meaning behind them.

Brands must build a relationship to succeed. Let's now look at the stages of brand engagement.

Romance: focus on discovery and attraction

- Engage them in a mission of discovery via posted activity or recommendation from a friend.
- Grab their attention (unique 'shareable' and 'fresh' messages).
- Do not spam ... ever.
- 'The ideal interaction between me and the brand is the one I ask for.'
- 'I follow the brands because my friends suggest them to me, but I am not interested in all the brands.'
- 'I love seeing things behind the scene.'

Familiarization: create intimacy and build credentials via humanization

- Promise a uniquely informative or fun experience based on personal preferences.
- Incentivize with exclusive offerings.
- Lots of fans/followers are indicative of ability to satisfy.
- 'I think that for me to become a fan of a brand, it would have to give me interesting and relevant content. For example, I love football, and I follow the Nike football page. Why? Because they post incredible videos about football that I love watching.'
- 'I think the issue companies are disregarding is: who is behind the brand? ... Apple is Jobs and Microsoft is Gates ... For a company to have charisma, it needs people. And to relate, it has to be to someone, not something.'

- Consumers want interaction with experts, not amateurs.
- 'These people have to be someone of extreme confidence in the company, as it is a spokesperson with great power in his or her hands. Companies are tempted to hire very junior people to be responsible for the social networks, when it should be exactly the opposite.'

Power struggle: cultivate trust through transparency and consistency

- Must share information and let them decide.
- Engage in real time to demonstrate empathy and responsiveness.
- 'I expect the brand's Facebook (page) to be transparent enough that it does not remove the negative posts or block the writer of the negative post. It should be candid enough to expect both bouquets and brickbats.'
- 'I know a few small businesses on Facebook that are well trusted and have over a thousand fans because they don't try and scam anybody, they don't have any gimmicks, and they're honest about their products and services.'

Stability: behave less like a brand and more like a friend

- Create a dialogue.
- The more invested they are in the brand, the more likely they are to support it.
- Seek their input for co-creation.
- Create a sense of ownership.
- Offer something without asking for something in return or 'selling'.
- 'What works with me is two-sided interaction – the brand speaks but it wants to listen to me. You have to feel like part of the brand information, that's what makes a difference in social networks.'
- 'On Twitter, I follow Speedo ... there are always quite useful sports and food tips ... it's a win-win situation. They "help" me and I help them by purchasing on their website and re-tweeting the cool tips.'

Some brands are getting it:

Romance: China: Meizhiyuan Orange Juice integrated the brand in social farming game prior to launch. United Kingdom: PG tips grabs attention by showcasing its main TV character in a fun and entertaining way.

Familiarization: United Kingdom: Apple's iPod Facebook application gives latest news on entertainment; something for everyone.

Power struggle: Colombia: Sipote Burrito uses 'first person tweets' to address problems, answer questions and fill requests. United Kingdom: Love film.com uses Twitter and iPhone application as an easier and faster method of collecting and delivering personal information.

Stability: South Africa: Woolworths' Facebook page for continuous dialogue; addresses interests and questions.

We have found lots of global commonalities, and only a few differences between continents and countries.

People from South Africa to the United States to Colombia find the same appeal in social media and derive similar benefits from it. After all, those deep-seated emotional drivers operate on a human level (versus a cultural one). However, there are a few notable differences. China is an interesting case because the government tightly controls the flow of information. The Chinese people we spoke to have been quick to embrace social media but have yet to fully experience some of the applications and platforms. For example, access to Facebook is strictly prohibited. They have other social networks such as RenRen that serve the same end, but they feel left out of the global conversation without the ability to use Facebook. They have friends and colleagues who live and work outside China and know what's available – and what they are missing. Controls on sites like Facebook run counter to the freedom they believe is inherent in social media.

India also has a strong desire to fully join the global community on social media but for slightly different reasons. Indians are undergoing a shift in their social networking preferences from the well-established platform, Orkut, to Facebook. They feel Orkut is not evolving fast enough – and with enough innovative features and functionality – to keep up with what people are looking for from social media platforms. In addition, Orkut feels 'dated' and too rooted in the region and, more specifically, the developing world. Thus, more and more Indians have moved to Facebook as their primary social network.

In short, social media is indeed a powerful force in the world. It has reshaped the way we interact with one another, how consumers look at brands and, in turn, how brands will need to act to capture the attention and loyalty of consumers. If brands are to succeed in social media, they must change their entire marketing approach:

- act like a friend, not a corporation;
- build relationships with consumers rather than 'sell';
- think community not marketplace.

As a respondent told us, '[Brands] have to surprise me, not only meet my needs, but anticipate my needs. By using social media exclusively, I think the company has to answer me whenever I have a question, enlighten me whenever I complain, and thank me whenever I compliment them.' If brands can do that – by speaking the right language in social media – they will undoubtedly find lots of consumer love.

I have had the opportunity to read closely the study we did on Spain regarding this subject (thank you and congratulations to Rosana Rodríguez and Diana Regidor). I am going to comment on some of its main conclusions below.

New generations come equipped with a 'digital' brain. Social media is growing exponentially every day. Users spend between 50 and 80 minutes a day on the network. Why? Because:

- it is a new way of relating to others and it is creating new motivation;
- within current society there is a strong desire to be the protagonist;
- there is a strong sense of exhibitionism: diaries used to be private, now they are flashed around openly;
- they are looking to live life intensely: social media allows them to have the whole world within arm's reach;
- it is efficient: with a simple 'click' (minimum effort) the user becomes a 'crack' (maximum reward).

Four different types of relationships have been established with social media: proactive, receptive, indifferent and hostile.

The study tells us that, roughly speaking, brands are disorientated within social media. Many brands have missed the bus when it comes to social networks. Until recently a brand was like a 'symbolic conversation' with the consumer, but everything has changed. Now it is a real, direct conversation. Brands feel uncomfortable in this new world, and act as if social media is a sort of shifting sand. The initial temptation is to use the same tools as for traditional marketing, but the social media environment requires new ways of approaching and interacting with consumers. Great care is needed because we are at a point where the consumer is becoming much more credible than the brands. Consumers' opinions about the various products and services on the market are competing with the brands' advertising campaigns. Because of these changes, the senior executives of a company often do not make it easy for that company and its brands to break into social media.

The keys for brands are as follows:

- This is the time to interact: this phenomenon of 'empowerment' of social media users has to be harnessed.
- Commit to using social media: passion, involvement, involvement of management, and hiring a community manager.
- Appropriate follow-ups: go to and be present where the brand's target audience is.

- Dare to take part: to have an impact, be surprising and interesting in an original way.

- The values that guarantee success are still authenticity, honesty and transparency, to be able to achieve the glittering prize that is credibility with the user.

- To be constantly close to the users, or even ahead of them. This may be where the new trends are.

- Social media is a very special 'party' and brands have not been invited. If you turn up unannounced you have to take a 'gift' (useful hints and tips for consumers, promotions, offers, events, etc).

- You have to turn 'buzzing' into 'jazz': namely, transform negative network 'noise' into music for the brand. It means creating a pleasant melody about the brand that can reach the ears of the consumer.

Brands in the social media

A few days after the publication of the study on the 100 most valuable global brands, in May 2011, *The Financial Times* dedicated a section to this topic.

The last paragraph about the subject of social media was entitled 'It is important not to invade others' space', written by Jessica Twentyman. I have reproduced Jessica's work below, because it is based on the conclusions of this Millward Brown survey, and also because it is a good analysis of the current situation within social media.

Listening not shouting can avert a lot of damage.

In the 'real' world, acceptable social behaviour is typically defined by a set of conventions that most people learn from childhood onwards.

In most cultures, it is considered discourteous to interrupt a conversation between strangers without introducing yourself, distinctly impolite to impose a new topic of conversation on that group and down-right boorish to talk about one's self without listening to what others have to say.

In the online world of social networks, businesses flout these rules all the time – but the repercussions are just the same, warns Peter Walshe, global BrandZ director at Millward Brown: 'They either get laughed at or frozen out.'

'The problem,' he says, 'is that because social media represent a relatively cost-effective channel for promoting a brand, there is a tendency for businesses to leap in without learning the rules of etiquette.

'That is a pity,' he adds, 'because brands that conduct themselves with aplomb on social networks – offering relevant input when appropriate, but more often simply taking careful note of the feedback they are offered – have much to gain. Those that do not, by contrast, run the risk of serious brand damage.'

'It is not just a question of how a brand interacts with its target audience online, however. An even trickier challenge is working out why it should do so at all,' says Clay Shirky, the social media commentator and author. 'You have a bunch of marketing people out there telling their bosses that their company must start a blog, or set up a Facebook fan page or a Twitter account – but when they're asked what the value might be, they tend to go a little quiet,' he says.

'If Mr Shirky's 2008 bestseller *Here Comes Everybody* alerted many companies worldwide to the breadth and depth of online conversations that consumers were holding, his new book, *Cognitive Surplus*, underscores the huge potential value of those conversations, not just for consumers but for the businesses and public-sector organizations that serve them, too. Above all,' he concludes, 'success is often a question of observing the conversational etiquette of "listening, not shouting".'

For the world's leading brands, there is a lot of listening to be done. In an effort to pin down the often fuzzy correlation between online conversations and brand value, BrandZ recently engaged global market intelligence company Cymphony to screen more than 3,400 million documents for relevant online mentions in 2010 of brands listed on the BrandZ top 100 Most Valuable Global Brands.

'In total,' says Mr Walshe, '125 million mentions of the Top 100 brands were discovered – or four mentions per second. To impose some kind of qualitative assessment on that data, 91 million documents were selected for further analysis, and a final, multilanguage dataset was assessed for sentiment – positive, neutral or negative – using natural language processing (NLP) technology.

'We then created a "Buzz Index" for each brand on the listing, where the average is 100,' Mr Walshe explains. 'Mentions were upgraded if sentiment was positive and downgraded where negatively biased, using a "Positivity Score", where positive counted 2, neutral 0 and negative minus 1.'

A brand's 'Buzz Score' (also an average of 100) was multiplied by the 'Positive Score' to produce the Buzz Index. 'The resulting Buzz Index shows some relationship between brand value and positive online buzz, but it is not absolute,' Mr Walshe warns.

'The more buzz a brand creates does not necessarily equate to higher brand value, because the truth is that some (industry) categories are simply more "buzzable" than others, as are some brands,' he says.

That is certainly true of technology companies, which attract the most online comment, occupying seven of the top 10 Buzz Index slots. In first place is Google, the search engine company, with Facebook only a little behind.

There is also little correlation between the buzz a brand creates and its overall financial value – suggesting, perhaps, that smaller companies have as much to play for in the social networking realm as their larger counterparts.

What is clear is that even brands from sectors that are frequently viewed in a negative light can still create a positive buzz.

Of the three other top 10 slots in the Buzz Index, two of the brands, Germany's BMW and Honda of Japan are from the automotive sector – an industry that attracts some of the highest volumes of criticism online, along with soft drinks and fast food.

'Even though your category may be viewed in a negative light, perhaps for reasons to do with environmental or health concerns, social networking offers an opportunity to rise above the general perception and elevate a brand in the eyes of target audiences.' says Mr Walshe.

So what can brand managers learn from the Buzz Index in terms of their online behaviour? Mr Walshe's advice is clear: listen and learn. 'Don't interrupt a social space,' he says. 'Recognize that the space belongs to other people not to you and your brand.'

Table 14.4 shows the world's 10 leading brands and their relation to the buzz they create on social media.

TABLE 14.4 Buzz Index Top 10 (2010)

Rank	Brand	Buzz Index	Positivity
1	Google	1,733	95
2	Facebook	1,184	91
3	Microsoft	742	102
4	Apple	704	93
5	Sony	433	97
6	BMW	366	87
7	BlackBerry	330	106
8	Walmart	325	97
9	Samsung	314	108
10	Honda	307	88

MillwardBrown
Optimor

Summary of key learning points about brands

- Whenever we are about to launch a new brand, a new product or service onto the market, whenever we test a new concept, we have to take into account how it stacks up against the following characteristics: originality and innovation; degree of attractiveness (level of aspiration); ease of use; usefulness (functionality); and price (it must be reasonable and it must be good value for money).

- This simple template is a good predictor of the level of success a brand will have. If it complies closely with each and every one of these requirements, we can think in terms of good business. But if it does not, it would be advisable to have a rethink and start improving on the idea.

- Nigel Hollis and Gordon Pincott have developed a model for analysing the success of a brand in the market. This 'Value Drivers Model' has been developed as a framework to help clients identify how best to grow the value of their brand. The model consists of two basic steps. 1) Define: What does the brand offer that is meaningfully different from other brands in the category? 2) Amplify: How best can that difference be amplified across the brand experience?

- Defining a meaningfully different experience: people choose brands that they find to be meaningfully different, a perception that creates a desire to buy the brand.

- Clarity of purpose: why does the brand exist? Purpose refers to the difference a brand intends to make in people's brains/minds/lives.

- Delivery: having a clear purpose for the brand is important, but the brand must then live up to its purpose. Ideally a brand should deliver an outstanding experience.

- Consumer resonance: for the brand's offer to be meaningful and valuable it must resonate with the target consumer.

- Competitive offer: whether a brand offers something different can only be defined in the competitive context.

- Amplification includes:
  - Findability: physical availability is vital to the success of a brand.
  - Affordability: the interaction of price and meaningful difference is a major consideration in growing value.
  - Extendability: a major way of growing brand value is by extending a brand that has been successful in one country into other countries (or categories).
  - Credibility: it is important that the brand behaves in a way that aligns with the experience it offers in every way in which it appears to its customers.
  - Vitality: it is crucial that a brand is seen to be alive and active, a brand that is both popular and contemporary.

- The secrets of the most valuable global brands:
  - Consumers' minds: listening closely to them; talking to them; anticipating change; understanding change; acting as soon as possible (faster than their competitors); offering features and functions relevant to consumers.
  - The product: innovating (easy to say, difficult to achieve); investing in originality (novelty and innovation captures the mind's attention); creating a good brand experience (having satisfied customers); fulfilling the brand's promise (feeling of trust and credibility); offering value at a reasonable price (fair).
  - Communications: clarity and impact, because this makes it easier to understand and remember messages; openness and transparency, because this creates credibility; create confidence; being honest; measure communications activities in the real and the digital world (social networks).
  - The brand: differentiation; consistency in the brand's essence and strategy, but at the same time having a margin for manoeuvre (flexibility); breaking the rules in the present to create a future; corporate social responsibility (CSR): a sincere commitment, relevant to the consumer and coherent with the essence of the brand.

- Key things to remember about social media:
  - Act like a friend not a corporation.
  - Build a relationship rather than sell.
  - Think community not marketplace.

Millward Brown and neuroscience

15

> *To know how to wonder and question is the first step of the mind toward discovery!*
> **LOUIS PASTEUR**

The Branded Mind

I have just finished reading the new book written by my colleague Erik Du Plessis, *The Branded Mind: What neuroscience really tells us about the puzzle of the brain and the brand* (Kogan Page and Millward Brown, 2011) and I recommend that you read it too.

Brain science has undergone a revolution. It features on the front pages of magazines and the work of brain scientists is regularly reported in popular books and newspapers. At the same time, 'neuromarketing', a term only coined in 2002, is now a hot topic and freely used in the marketing media. But how does the application of neuroscience affect established market research techniques? Could neuroscience learn from existing methodologies?

In *The Branded Mind* Erik du Plessis sets out to answer these questions. He explores what we know about the structure of the brain, explaining how the different parts of the brain interact and the roles emotions, moods, personality and culture play in our lives. He then demonstrates how this relates to current theories on consumer behaviour, exploring the impact of longer-lasting feelings on decision making and brand allegiance. Erik then explores some implications for practitioners of both marketing and neuroscience, investigating how brain science can contribute to marketing and brand-building strategies.

Chapter 18 of the book is called 'Increasing our brainpower – using neuroscience effectively'. It was written by Graham Page (Millward Brown Executive Vice-President, Consumer Neuroscience). This is what Graham has to say at the beginning of the chapter:

Erik's book illustrates both the complexity of neuroscience as a field, and the crucial implications it has for brand owners as they seek to make their brands more desirable to consumers and win in the marketplace. It is, therefore, unsurprising that marketing and advertising conferences now incorporate a strong neuroscience emphasis, and many recent papers and articles maintain that scientists' increased understanding of the brain will change marketing and the way we measure it. 'Buy-ology', by Martin Lindstrom, makes similarly strong claims: that neuroscience will play a revolutionary role in research and marketing in future. As a result, many marketers challenge accepted modes of brand and advertising development and research on the grounds that 'neuroscience says' that what we've done before is wrong.

Similarly, we now see neuroscience being cited in many brand and advertising decisions. The phrase 'neuroscience proves ...' is increasingly being used to justify a new model of advertising response, brand strategy or advertising research tool (though it's often useful to examine just how much actual proof follows such statements). Most crucially, over the last few years there has been a blossoming of neuromarketing agencies who claim to deploy the methods used by neuroscientists to answer marketing questions in a way that conventional research cannot.

So we'd be forgiven for believing that traditional qualitative (focus group-based) and quantitative (survey-based) techniques are not sufficient anymore, and that we need to turn to the methods used by cognitive neuroscientists, such as brainwave measurement (EEG), brain scanning (MRI) and other biometrics, to really understand how consumers will respond to marketing.

However, despite all the discussion about neuroscience, the vast majority of brands and ads are still researched using traditional methods. Likewise, papers have periodically emerged that question the value of the whole area. So who's right? Are we poised at the start of a revolution or is neuromarketing overhyped wishful thinking?

Graham continues discussing the current state of play:

Millward Brown conducted its first neuroscience project in 2004, and since then we have reviewed all the key methodologies available in this area, working with our clients, neuromarketing practitioners and academics. Our experience is that marketers are increasingly turning to neuromarketing, and they will continue to do so more and more in future. But this has been a gradual process for several reasons:

1 Marketers are rightly cautious. Neuromarketing is new and to some people controversial. So they are working with partners who they trust to do their homework before adopting more widely.

2 There are still significant practical hurdles. The technologies are not available everywhere, and the logistics of brainwave measurements or brain scanning are not trivial. Testing robust numbers of participants is often expensive – or worse, not done.

3 The extreme claims of some of the early practitioners in the field have inspired some scepticism.

4 Many of our clients believe their work in this area has the potential to generate significant competitive advantage, and so are understandably coy about sharing too much publicly.

5 Most marketers quickly realize that neuroscience methods in isolation can be hard to interpret and don't stand alone.

This last point is crucial. Over the last six years we have examined all the main techniques in the area and compared them to the existing qualitative and quantitative work we do to ensure a realistic perspective on what the science can and can't say. We've seen that there is clear and significant value in certain neuroscience methods, but only when used alongside existing methods rather than as a replacement, and only if interpreted with care by people with experience in the field. To this end, in 2010 we created a dedicated Neuroscience Practice to ensure that, as a business, we would implement neuroscience-based approaches in a realistic manner that added to our insights about consumers.

These words of Graham's are a very good expression of my own thoughts on this new knowledge tool.

Improving our brainpower

The market research world has a suite of powerful techniques, both quantitative (survey-based interviewing) and qualitative (flexible techniques like group discussions or more developmental work). Neuroscience is beginning to offer some new possibilities. We can, for instance, show people a brand and directly measure what goes on in their brains, missing out the messy business of questions and interviews. The future is now! It will not, however, completely replace conventional research any time soon. There are some issues:

- *Ethics:* initial studies in the United States were met with a lot of controversy. This is unfounded. The techniques measure, they don't brainwash. The only difference between this and conventional research is that people can't 'lie' to us as easily. It is an implicit measure; the consumer doesn't have to make an oral statement. This is just another way to try to improve campaign effectiveness. If that's unethical, so is conventional ad research.

- *Hype:* there is a lot of 'over-claim' in this area. These techniques are meaningful, but what they show is which areas of the brain light up in response to stimuli. What that means is down to interpretation. Also, the measures are still crude. In terms of emotional response, it can measure positive and negative, but nuance requires conventional research. Notably we find that outcomes from our surveys align well with neuroscience results.

- *Practicality:* this can be expensive. The situation can be clinical. The sample sizes are often small. The techniques work with small numbers but there are still potential issues with generalizability from small samples.

- *Neuroscience is a useful addition, not a replacement:* because of this, focusing too much on the techniques risks missing the point. This is why we will focus on how neuroscience can provide additional insight when used alongside our current offering.

The combination of conventional research methods and neuroscience gives us the best of both worlds: robust, established explicit techniques with a proven track record, combined with implicit methods that give incremental insight into motivation and perceptions. The main benefits are:

- We provide an integrated picture – clients (marketers) don't have to piece it together.

- We've done the homework on the techniques and what the science means – clients don't have to work it out.

- We only deploy implicit techniques when they add value – there is no wastage.

- We're not wedded to one method or technology – we will deploy the right tools for the job, alongside our existing methods.

After testing multiple technologies, the type of research we are currently carrying out within Millward Brown is focused on the use of three methods:

1 Brainwave measurement (EEG): understanding the moment-by-moment response to brand communications and experiences.

2 Eye-tracking: understanding the focus of visual attention within campaigns.

3 Implicit association measurement: understanding the associations and emotional responses generated by brands and ads.

Why have we chosen these three methods? Because they are the only ones that have provided a positive response to the following questions:

- Do the techniques yield meaningful results?

- Do they deliver incremental insights? Enough to justify the cost?

- Are they better predictors of behaviour than existing approaches?

There are certain situations in which these techniques are particularly useful:

- Dealing with sensitive material that might provoke a socially unacceptable response.

- Exploring an ad communication that is implied rather than shown or said.

- Exploring implicit brand associations – especially higher order or abstract values.
- Diagnostics, for example measuring transient responses that have a bigger effect when people tell us the story of an ad.
- Investigating emotion.
- Exploring general questions about how marketing 'works'.
- Adding the 'wow' factor.

None of the techniques makes sense in isolation; we need an holistic approach to understand them. It's all about integration.

The contributions of neuroscience to marketing research

EEG

EEG (brainwave measurement) is a modern, functional and simple technology that consists of putting a comfortable band around a person's head and recording the brain's electrical activity as he or she watches a stimulus. As you can see in Figure 15.1, the equipment involves a simple headband (like the sort used by tennis players).

FIGURE 15.1

The EEG offers several advantages:

- technology optimized for market research rather than biomedical research;
- it is practical and scale-able;
- wireless and mobile;
- easily transferred across locations;
- integrates with conventional research;
- it is cost-effective.

We have used EEG technology for TV advertisements, print and auditory stimuli. We have also bought eye-tracking equipment from the Tobii company. Externally, it looks very similar to a computer screen and is very user-friendly. It can be used to determine where the people's visual attention is drawn when they are watching the stimulus. Figure 15.2 shows the Tobii eye-tracker being used.

FIGURE 15.2

Eye-tracking technology:

- is non-invasive;
- is portable;
- has fast calibration;
- tracks both eyes allowing freedom of movement;
- can track people wearing glasses.

Eye-tracking has different applications, including advertising development research, concept testing, logo and pack design, online usability, micro-site development and in-store marketing (dynamic equipment).

Brainwave measurement (EEG)

Let's now focus on what EEG can offer market research. The basics are:

- It is the oldest method of studying the brain's functioning (approximately 100 years).
- Electrodes placed on the scalp record the electrical activity of the brain.
- The recorded signal is a measurement of currents that flow during synaptic excitations of the dendrites of many pyramidal neurons in the cerebral cortex.

Features of EEG:

- Poor spatial resolution: the exact source of activity cannot be defined precisely.
- Excellent temporal resolution (ms scale): activity changes in response to fast-changing stimuli can be tracked.
- Records only cortical activity.
- Can be used to record fine temporal changes in brain activity of relatively big cortical structures (eg prefrontal or parietal cortex).
- Cognitive response: less alpha in prefrontal cortex, more cognitive engagement, more thinking: higher cognitive functions (planning, reasoning, problem solving): decisions.
- Emotional response: left/right asymmetry in alpha power in prefrontal cortex related to approach/withdrawal: more activation in the left prefrontal cortex = approach; more activation in the right prefrontal cortex = withdrawal.

Figure 15.3 is a representation of the emotional response in the prefrontal cortex.

FIGURE 15.3

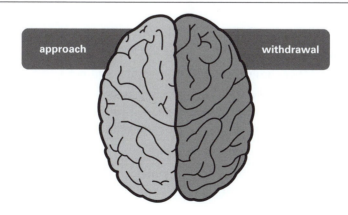

The types of metrics and the features that make it suitable for use in market research are:

- Scene study including emotional response to scenes, cognitive response to scenes, and scene synchronicity.
- Scapes (brand, character, others).
- Emotional and cognitive traces.
- Indicators of efficacy: engagement efficiency, brand/product response, emotional trend, key points of cognition, and audience synchronicity.
- Specifically designed for market research:
  - dry electrodes, wireless, mobile, captures brainwaves and respiration, blinking, head movement, temperature and changes in heart rate;
  - quick set-up;
  - samples of over 100 consumers;
  - testing in several locations.

We usually use this method with an explicit technique (quantitative or qualitative interview), with N = 150 and time: viewing time of an ad plus a few minutes for calibration.

To summarize, recording the brain's electrical activity allows us to analyse, photogram by photogram, the emotions generated by the communication activity (both positive and negative), as well as the cognitive activity (thought) triggered in the consumer's mind.

EEG: Lech beer case study

We are next going to look at an analysis of a television ad campaign for Lech beer (SAB Miller) in Poland. The ad is called 'Helicopters' and lasts 45 seconds.

The action starts on the roof terrace of a tall building in the centre of a modern city. A group of people suddenly rush onto the terrace towards a group of helicopters, which have arrived to rescue the people. The urgency and the noise of the rotors and the helicopters' engines convey the idea of lots of action in the various scenes (kicking open the door to the roof, running on to rooftop, helicopter, long shot of rooftop).

The camera focuses on a couple. They have a son. The man tells the woman to take the baby:

Man: 'I'm not going.'
Woman: 'Why?'
Man: 'There are people in this town that still need me.'

The man wipes a tear from the woman's cheek. They kiss intensely. Another helicopter flies by. She gets on board. She is carrying the baby in her arms. The man shouts instructions to the pilot from the roof terrace.

Man: 'And don't call me before 2 pm.'

The man makes a movement with his hands, imitating the rotors of the helicopter. The situation moves suddenly from action to a brief comic, ironic

FIGURE 15.4 'Spot' cerveza en Polonia

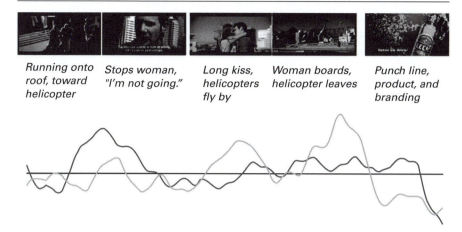

| Running onto roof, toward helicopter | Stops woman, "I'm not going." | Long kiss, helicopters fly by | Woman boards, helicopter leaves | Punch line, product, and branding |

moment. The helicopters are seen drawing away. Images of a glass and Lech beer appear.

> Voice off camera: 'And what do you do with your family on Friday evening?'

A banner appears across the screen: 'Lech: it starts!'

Figure 15.4 shows consumer responses to the ad. We have to analyse the communication activity scene by scene. The green line shows the progression of emotions, while the blue line shows the thought level.

EEG delivers deep insight into the impact of marketing communications on consumers by capturing emotional responses and cognitive thought measurements. Positive/negative emotion: when do viewers feel positive and negative emotions? Cognitive thought: when do viewers mentally engage and process information?

Overall, this ad performs above average on key indicators of efficacy, with two out of five performing above the study average: The spot elicits a strong cognitive response as audiences work out what is happening, leading to an above average score on key points of cognition. Brand/product performance, though mixed, is driven to above average levels by the positive emotions and high cognition regarding the Lech bottle.

The narrative of the spot is highly engaging, from the tension of the man deciding not to leave to the long slow-motion kiss: The initial scenes cause negative emotions, as viewers figure out what's going to happen. The kiss elicits strong positive emotions. The scene of many helicopters flying overhead is the emotional climax of the ad.

The performance of the final scenes in which the product is introduced, however, does not perform as strongly: The written line, 'And what do you do with your family on a Friday evening?' as well as 'Lech: it starts!' both elicit negative emotions.

Flow of emotion: audiences respond positively to the long kiss and the helicopters flying overhead. The punch line, product, and branding, however, fail to drive similarly strong positive emotions. The negative emotions during the couple's conversation suggest tension, relating to danger or an unknown threat. The helicopter's departure creates positive emotions, because the mother and baby are safe. But the appearance of the product, the glass and the brand don't create positive emotions; quite the contrary in fact.

Flow of cognition: cognition spikes shortly into the spot, as audiences are shown the helicopter and are able to piece together what is happening. High cognition indicates that viewers are thinking intensely about the scenes, trying to figure out or anticipate what's going to happen.

Dialogue moments with positive emotions:

'Lech.'

Dialogue moments with negative emotions:

'I'm not going'

'Why?'

'Hold on to Jacusia!' (the name of the baby)

'And what do you do with your family on a Friday evening?'

'Lech: it starts!'

Audience synchronicity is highest when the woman asks the question, 'Why?' It is also generally elevated in scenes with helicopters flying overhead.

The campaign created interest and tension right from the beginning. It unleashes intense emotional and cognitive responses. However, there is a very strong contrast between the situation the ad sets out and the final resolution. The action is so real and believable that it is then difficult to incorporate the humorous twist introduced when the woman and child leave, the ironic dimension to the message and the arrival of the product and the brand.

This analysis (EEG) allows us to see the efficacy of communication, the points of greatest connection with the viewer and to focus on the scenes where the brand and the product appear. In this way we can carry out an in-depth diagnosis of the campaign and better predict its impact on consumers. It also offers us the opportunity to edit or change those scenes that contribute least towards the campaign's objectives. It is increasingly important to use tools that help manufacturers (marketers) and creative directors to understand how the final product works.

Eye-tracker

First, a little background about eye movement:

- Visual acuity is highest at the fixation point.
- Thus, eye movements are necessary to analyse the entire scene.

- Eye movements = fixations + saccades (quick, simultaneous movements of both eyes in the same direction).
- Scene analysis takes place only during fixations.
- The longer the fixation time, the more complex the cognitive processing.
- Fixations take place in informative areas of the visual scene.
- Eye-mind hypothesis: eye movements reflect visual attention allocation.

Eye-tracking technology records eye movements and the eye position is imposed on the scene. It works as follows:

- Eye trackers use infrared light to generate reflection patterns on the user's corneas.
- On the basis of these reflection patterns, a gaze point on the screen can be calculated.
- Respondent watches the tested material while his other eye movements are recorded by the eye-tracker.
- One or several screens.
- Time: viewing time of the material + few minutes for calibration.
- N = 30 per 1 heatmap; if alternative versions tested, 30 respondents for each version needed.
- Quantitative output: heatmaps, clusters, numerical data.
- Possibility of generalizing the results.
- It is advisable to complement this with a qualitative stage.

An eye-tracker can:

- Tell whether or not users are looking at the screen.
- Differentiate reading from scanning for particular words or phrases.
- Learn the relative intensity of a user's attention to various parts of an image (which elements are most salient, interesting or difficult to understand).
- Compare users' overall scan patterns (successive saccades and fixations).
- Provide numerical, measurable and objective data, which might show other results.
- Let you know whether users actually 'see' something (the respondent might have been looking at something but did not register it).
- Prove that users did not see something (users can acquire information through peripheral vision).
- Determine why users are looking at something.
- Record people's behaviour, but interpretation has to be done by you.
- Test everybody (including those with strong glasses, bifocal glasses, a squint or extensive blinking).

There are different versions of eye-tracking. The first and perhaps best known is similar to a computer screen: excellent for testing anything that can be put on a monitor. The second version, not limited by a monitor, can measure anything that can remain in a defined area for the time of the test. The third is in the form of a pair of glasses, which make it easier for the consumer to move around. This is ideal for ethnology studies at points of sale.

Eye-tracking is an implicit methodology: it does not require the consumer to make a statement. Therefore, it is a good complement to qualitative research (explicit focus). Individuals may not be fully aware of all the aspects that influence their visual perception and in being able to decode a stimulus.

In an experiment, two identical stimuli were show to two sample groups of test subjects. The two groups were made up of people with the same characteristics in terms of their classification (age, gender, etc). The stimuli shown to both groups comprised two landscapes. One of them showed a train accident – a scene that captured the participants' attention and generated negative emotions. The other landscape, which was a picture of a forest, showed a fairly neutral situation in terms of the emotions it generated, neither positive nor negative.

Figure 15.5 shows the two images used during this experiment. The first group were told to look at the image of the train; the results obtained are

FIGURE 15.5

FIGURE 15.6 Look at the image of the train

shown in Figure 15.6. As you can see, practically the whole group focused their visual attention on the train accident.

But the results were quite different when the second group were told to look at the forest landscape; see Figure 15.7.

The result was that a good number of the sample concentrated their visual attention on the train accident, because the information was much more relevant. Despite the fact that these people were given a very clear oral instruction, their visual attention moved towards another image.

FIGURE 15.7 Look at the forest landscape

Eye-tracker: Dolce & Gabbana case study

This research, like the other case studies here, was carried out using the Tobii eye-tracker. The first example is a static advertising campaign (magazines, shelters, advertising hoardings, etc) for the brand Dolce & Gabbana and its fragrance, Light Blue, which has versions for men and for women. The sample was made up of 60 people: 30 men and 30 women, aged between 25 and 40.

First we will look at the message for the men's fragrance, which appears in Figure 15.8.

FIGURE 15.8

The results from eye-tracking are shown in Figure 15.9. The eye-tracker's main output is in the form of a heat map, showing the fixation points of the eye and of attention, as well as the length of time (permanence) the gaze remains there, using a colour code (the deeper the red the greater the permanence).

Consumers' visual perception centres on the triangle, then the model's face, name of fragrance, bottle. This is, therefore, a fairly effective campaign. The visual trajectory moves from the man's face to the name or the bottle. The male face is the element that captures the greatest visual attention.

FIGURE 15.9

This technology allows us to establish the differences in perception between men and women, and between the visual attention of younger and older viewers. Figure 15.10 shows the differences between the male and female sample audiences. The results are very similar, but the women were a little more daring about where they looked than the men, and they also looked at the bottle more.

FIGURE 15.10

Men   Women

Next, we presented the consumer sample with the advertising campaign for the women's version of this product; see Figure 15.11.

FIGURE 15.11

This stimulus is less provocative than the previous one. The male version is more sexual and the female version is more sensual. Overall, the results are very similar to those we found for the men's version of the product. According to the results from the whole sample (men plus women) they looked slightly more at the woman's body than that of the man.

FIGURE 15.12

But, if we look at the analysis separating the data according to gender, we can see that the male viewers show greater interest in the sexual areas of the female model. They also look more at the model's face and the name of the product (Light Blue).

FIGURE 15.13

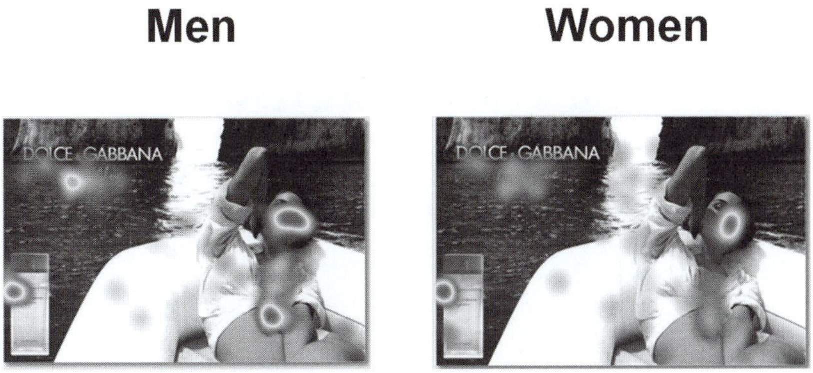

We have seen two good examples of effective static advertising. The creative director has used few visual stimuli, but ones that are very relevant: the model, the brand, the name of the product and the packaging. This simplicity makes it easy for the consumer to visually decode and receive the message.

Eye-tracker: Euphoria (Calvin Klein) case study

Let's now look at another example of women's fragrance. It also involves a printed campaign for magazines, shelters and advertising hoardings.

Eye-tracker: Santander-Ferrari case study

Let's look at another example of applying eye-tracking to print advertising (static campaigns) intended for newspapers, magazines, advertising hoardings, shelters, etc. It is a campaign for Banco Santander and Ferrari.

A significant claim is made in the upper part of the piece; it says: 'The podium wears red.' In the lower half are two very famous Formula 1 racing drivers: Fernando Alonso and Felipe Massa, drivers for the Ferrari team at the time of this campaign. In the upper left you can see the Ferrari logo and centre right the logo for Banco Santander, (and its claim, 'The value of ideas'); see Figure 15.14.

FIGURE 15.14

The objective of this campaign was to show the association between the brands Santander and Ferrari.

The same sample as the previous advertising messages was used. An analysis of the results from the eye-tracking exercise shows that this is a clear and well-constructed message, consisting of only a few elements: the two drivers, the two logos and the claim (all revolving around the colour red). It clearly conveys the message: successful drivers supported by successful brands. It produces a good level of complementarity between the car (Ferrari), the drivers (Fernando Alonso and Felipe Massa) and the sponsoring brand (Santander). Figure 15.15 shows the results provided by eye-tracking.

The visual perception of those taking part in the experiment allowed us to catalogue the different communications elements according to their importance:

1 The claim, 'The podium wears red', immediately below the face of Fernando Alonso. The claim is reminiscent of the headlines in a sporting newspaper.

2 The Santander logo (close to Alonso's face) and the face of Felipe Massa.

3 Finally, people looked towards the Ferrari logo.

FIGURE 15.15

The logo for Santander can be seen, but it could stand out much more, given its colour, but because it is on a red background it takes a little effort to spot it. The advertisement is a perfect triangular shape featuring the claim in the upper part (in red), the two racing drivers (in red) and the logo itself (also in red). But it would have been better to put the logo somewhere else so that it contrasts more with the background.

The analysis showed no major differences between the visual perception of the men and the women. The men looked at the Ferrari logo slightly more than the women did.

These examples of research carried out using eye-tracking show us how useful this technology can be in:

- having a better understanding of the impact of a specific print advertising campaign;
- making changes in order to optimize it;
- using what we have learnt to design future advertisements for the brand.

A glimpse of the future

Both electroencephalograms and eye-trackers are fascinating technological tools that complement and enrich the information offered by traditional market research, in both qualitative and quantitative terms.

The 21st century is going to be the century of the brain. Technology will continue its unstoppable advance and will allow us to follow the imprint left by communications, consumption and brand phenomena in consumers' minds. This is going to change the way markets are researched and researchers' activities. At the moment we are only at the beginning and we have to be both modest and optimistic about the results we can achieve.

At the same time, ethical standards are being developed to guarantee the confidentiality of information gleaned from consumers. All advances offer new opportunities and threats. Everything hangs on the intentions behind the use of these discoveries. The key is always the intention and significance of people's actions. It will be necessary to regulate the use of this technology to safeguard consumers' dignity and their freedom to choose when purchasing products.

Final reflections: philosophy and the mind

16

> "*It has been said that man is a rational animal. All my life
> I have been searching for evidence which could support this.*
>
> **BERTRAND RUSSELL**

The time has come to finish this book. We have now reached the final chapter, and I don't want to end without one more reference to Antonio Damasio.

One of the things that surprised me most about Damasio's research into the brain and mind was the connections he makes in his books (*Descartes' Error* and *Looking for Spinoza*) between neuroscience and philosophy. It was precisely this focus of Damasio's books that gave me the idea to end my own book by establishing a relationship between history's leading philosophers and the human mind.

Throughout the history of philosophical and scientific thought, the human mind has travelled many paths in an attempt to understand the enigmas involved in comprehending and interpreting the world that surrounds us. On some occasions thought has been downgraded in search of the sensory world (physical dimension); on others it has been elevated to the world of ideas (the metaphysical). Sometimes it has advanced towards a new view of the external reality; at other times it has gone backwards, because it needed to review aspects of the past and reinterpret them (re-view).

As regards what we have called 'downwards' orientation, there were currents of thought that highlighted the importance of feelings, perception, the senses, the physical world, events and experience. In these cases knowledge reverted to earthly matters and descended to the 'real' world (external and 'objective'). Here we have the nominalist (the individual case) and empiricist (experience) views.

There is also positivism, based on facts and the scientific method, closely bound to data and information. Within this perspective, the mind was essentially reduced to the level of sensations. This is precisely the position of David Hume, the 18th century Scottish philosopher, who took empiricism to the extreme, defending the fact that knowledge was mainly based on the senses. In this vein, thought was limited to sensations and perceptions. It cancelled out the role of reasoning.

In the other direction ('upwards') we have found schools that emphasized the role of reasoning and ideas. From this perspective knowledge was elevated to the heights and raised to the abstract world of concepts (the psyche, the internal and the 'subjective'). Here we find the idealism of Plato, the realist view of the problem of the 'universals' and the idealism of Hegel. In these perspectives the mind became synonymous with thinking and reasoning. And, sometimes, the senses were seen as a tool that deceives and confuses us.

According to the epistemologist Plato (idealist stance), the real truth lies in the world of ideas. Universal concepts are real. The real is what exists in the mind, and the environment that surrounds us is only an apparent reality. The physical world that reaches us through our senses is deceptive. The universals adopted a 'realist' posture that abstract concepts exist in reality.

In between these extremes are the balanced postures of Aristotle (observation plus mental categorization), the moderated realism of Boethius and Thomas Aquinas, the optimism of the Enlightenment, contributions from Kant (sensible thought plus intellectual thought; the 'thing-in-itself' plus the 'thing-in-me'), phenomenology, historicism, the integrationist view of Max Weber (historicism plus positivism), the approaches of Gadamer, Ricoeur, etc. These consist of a more integrated and holistic view of the human mind.

For Aristotle knowledge begins with the perception of the senses, thanks to which we understand the real aspects of things in the external world (colour, size, shape, etc). Then, a person's understanding goes through an abstraction process, capturing the true aspects of objects (their essence). Aristotle believed that human consciousness had 'the power of receiving into itself the sensible forms of things without the matter, in the way in which a piece of wax takes on the impress of a signet-ring without the iron or gold'. For Kant, 'All our knowledge begins with the senses, proceeds then to the understanding, and ends with reason.'

The mind is an assembly of very different and very advanced functions: impulses, sensations, perceptions, emotions, desires, expectations, intentions, intelligence, language, thought, beliefs, etc. Each one of us is the result of the interaction of all these functions.

The history of thought and ideas has advanced in a linear, dialectic and circular way, all at the same time. It is like a spiral rising upwards. It shows us multiple ways of understanding the world surrounding us. It is important to understand the different approaches because there is always something to learn from them. All encapsulate some 'truth' while each one has limitations and is incomplete. Each of them lays claim to having the full and definitive explanation about the mind and its relationship with the world.

Some authors have preferred the scientific method as a form of universal knowledge. Others believe that human and social sciences have to keep one eye on the scientific aspects and the other eye on more flexible methodologies that allow them to approach the objects of their study in a more holistic fashion (the individual, the mind, society, culture and the historical dimension). My way of thinking concurs with this second option.

Figure 16.1 is a graphical depiction of the integrated approach of the different schools of thought. On the left we have the world that surrounds

FIGURE 16.1

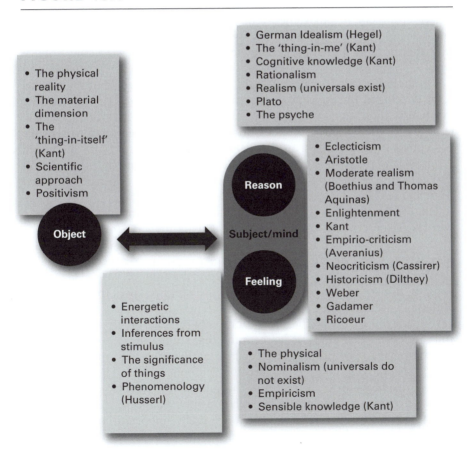

us, the external, 'objective' reality. It is the world of objects. It is the physical reality, the material dimension. Kant called this dimension the 'thing-in-itself', namely that our mind does not intervene; our optical vision is not in play. The philosophy of positivism pursues this objective. The scientific method always seeks this focus in an attempt to eliminate the influence of the human mind in relation to its environment as much as possible.

When an individual closes in on the external world things begin to happen. Interactions occur that entail exchanges of energy. The mind begins to create inferences from the stimuli that surround it. Eduardo Punset said that when one human being is close to another he or she always tries to guess that person's intentions using all the information he or she can gather from the situation. What is important is the significance of things. Husserl placed great importance on the phenomena created by interacting with the world (phenomenology).

When we get to subject (on the right of Figure 16.1), we have to distinguish between two levels: the mind seen from the senses, and the mind seen from the latest and most advanced evolutionary function – reasoning. The senses essentially connect us to the external world, to the physical world. We could say that the senses are more worldly. The senses relate to the environment through energy interactions. This is the sensible knowledge or perception that Kant talks about. Nominalism takes the same view (the specific and individual). Empiricism mainly emphasizes this subject level.

On the other side is reason. We are immersed in the world of the psyche. Kant developed the concept of the 'thing-in-me' for this side (namely, the external reality but now inside my mind). This perspective of the person takes us to what Kant called 'cognitive knowledge' (compared to sensible perception or knowledge). In this field we also find Plato (with his world of ideas), the realist posture in the problem of universals (in other words, that concepts exist in reality and are not mere abstract constructions) and German idealism, the leading exponent of which is Hegel.

Finally, the diagram shows us how all these philosophers overlap these two levels (perception and intellectual). This is the case for Aristotle, the moderate realism of Boethius and Thomas Aquinas, the Enlightenment, eclecticism, Kant, the empirio-criticism of Averanius, the neo-criticism of Cassirer, the historicism of Dilthey, the contributions of Weber, Gadamer, Ricoeur and so on. The modern view of the mind requires the integration of these two dimensions. At present, within human and social sciences, they have managed to break the dichotomy between the object being studied and the subject that analyses it (the mind that studies it).

People have been progressively distancing themselves from the physical reality and moving completely into the symbolic world. The meaning of things introduces us to the realm of the subject (the subjective dimension). Semantic chains evolve from the relationships between individuals and objects and with other subjects. What are really important are the significance of things and the intention of actions.

As an example, we will look at money. Its value changes depending on the people, the culture and the historical context. It involves a single, physical-material reality with many possible meanings. Money can be perceived as a means or an end in itself. It can be a means to achieve enjoyment and pleasure (hedonism). Money can be considered an expense or an investment. Money can be associated with the idea of saving in the sense of providing security and protection for the family, for example. For someone who invests money in the stock market, it can mean adventure, risk, etc. For anyone who plays the lottery, money is linked to chance and fortune (a magical dimension). Money can mean generosity when you share it with others. As we can see, the same reality can be lived in many different ways.

The reality that interests us is not the package of physical things, but the result of our relationship to them, namely the resulting cultural meanings and products. Perception is not exhausted in mere feelings. Consumers are not tied to 'things' (physical products), rather they move around like they are floating in the world of meanings that crop up in their relationship with elements of their environment.

As we have seen in this book, the consumer has senses and a mind. The senses take us towards the physical world of things. The mind takes us towards the meaning the world around us acquires, towards the field of semantics, towards the psychical reality. These are the relationships, the phenomena that 'things' create.

The consumer is a bio-psycho-socio-historical 'cell' and reading the reality of the marketplace is determined by these factors:

- The biological level: the influence of their body (genetics, biology, physiology, etc).
- The psychological plane: the influence of thought (the cognitive, the rational), of feelings (emotions, affection), of imagination (fantasy), of intentions, of desires, of experience, of beliefs, etc. The real drivers of our behaviour are our attitudes and beliefs (symbolic level).
- Social pressure: the social and cultural reality in which we are implanted determines our view of our surroundings.
- And finally, history: the historical stage (life stage) we are living through at any given time influences our relationship with the world that surrounds us.

But we are not alone. Every consumer has a particular relationship with the products in their external reality. And from these, they configure their internal, subjective reality. Our task as market researchers is to discover the acquired meaning of these products and brands for each of the consumers in our sample, and to arrive at the inter-subjective space where the majority of these consumers converge. Figure 16.2 shows the biological, psychological, sociological and historical influences on a person.

FIGURE 16.2

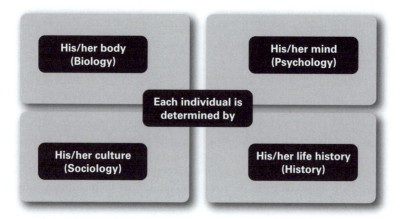

The philosopher Ortega y Gasset said that a person is 'I plus my circumstances.' Every consumer is determined by his or her circumstances, biological, psychological, sociological and historical. If we understand these circumstances, we will understand the 'why' of consumer habits.

The phenomena of consumption and the consumer mind are fascinating. Let's continue to deepen our understanding and move forward, but always in an ethical manner.

BIBLIOGRAPHY

Bassat, Luis: 'Inteligencia comercial', Plataforma editorial, 2011

Clark, David L, Boutros, Nashaat N y Méndez, Mario F: 'El cerebro y la conducta' (Neuroanatomía para psicólogos), Editorial Manual Moderno, 2005 (first published in English as The Brain and Behaviour: An introduction to behavioural neuroanatomy, Wiley-Blackwell, 2000)

Damasio, Antonio: 'El error de Descartes (la emoción, la razón y el cerebro humano)', Drakontos Bolsillo, 1994 (first published in English as Descartes' Error: Emotion, reason and the human brain, Putnam Publishing Group, 1994)

Damasio, Antonio: 'En busca de Spinoza (Neurobiología de la emoción y los sentimientos)', Drakontos, 2003 (first published in English as Looking for Spinoza: Joy, sorrow and the feeling brain, Harcourt Brace International, 2003)

Du Plessis, Eric: 'The advertised mind (ground-breaking insights into how our brains respond to advertising)', Kogan Page & Millward Brown, 2005

Du Plessis, Eric: 'The branded mind: What neuroscience really tells us about the puzzle of the brain and the brand)', Kogan Page & Millward Brown, 2011

Gladwell, Malcolm: 'Inteligencia intuitiva (¿Por qué sabemos la verdad en dos segundos?)', Ediciones Santillana, 2005 (first published in English as Blink. The power of thinking without thinking, 2005)

Goleman, Daniel: 'Inteligencia emocional', Editorial Kairós, 1995 (first published in English as Emotional Intelligence: Why it can matter more than IQ, Bantam Books, 1995)

Goleman, Daniel: 'Inteligencia social' (La nueva ciencia de las relaciones humanas), Editorial Kairós, 2006 (first published in English as Social Intelligence: The new science of human relationships, Bantam Books, 2006)

Graves, Philip: '¿Por qué consumimos? (El mito de los estudios de mercado, y las verdades sobre la psicología del comprador y su comportamiento)', Editorial Empresa Activa, 2011 (first published in English as Consumer.ology: The market research myth, the truth about consumers and the psychology of shopping, Nicholas Brealey, 2010)

Houdé, Olivier, Kayser, Daniel, Koening, Olivier, Proust, Joëlle y Rastier, François: 'Diccionario de ciencias cognitivas', Amorrortu editors, 2003 (first published in French as Vocabulaire de sciences cognitives. Neuroscience, psychologie, Intelligence artificielle, linguistique et philosophie,Presses Universitaires de France, 1998)

Jaúregui, José Antonio: 'Cerebro y emociones' (El ordenador emocional), 1998 (first published in English as The Emotional Computer, Wiley-Blackwell, 1995)

Johnson-Laird, P N: 'El ordenador y la mente', Editorial Paidós, 1990 (first published in English as The Computer and the Mind: Introduction to cognitive science, Harvard University Press, 1988)

Marina, José Antonio: 'El cerebro infantil: la gran oportunidad', Ariel, 2011

Mora, Francisco: 'Cómo funciona el cerebro', Alianza Editorial, 2009

Lindstrom, Martin: 'BRAND Sense. Build powerful brands through touch, taste, smell, sight and sound', Free Press, 2005

Lindstrom, Martin: *'Buy-ology (Verdades y mentiras de por qué compramos)'*, Grupo Editorial Norma, 2008 (first published in English as *Buyology: Truth and lies about why we buy*, Broadway Business, 2008)

Pinillos, José Luís: *'La mente humana'*, Editorial Círculo Universidad, 1998

Pinker, Steven: *'Cómo funciona la mente'*, Editorial Destino Imago Mundi, 1997 (first published in English as *How the Mind Works*, W W Norton & Co, 1997)

Punset, Eduardo: *'El viaje a la felicidad (las nuevas claves científicas)*, Editorial Destino, Imago Mundi, 2005 (first published in English as *The Happiness Trip, A scientific journey*, Chelsea Green Publishing, 2007)

Punset, Eduardo: *'El alma está en el cerebro' (Radiografía de la máquina de pensar)*, Editorial Aguilar, Biblioteca Redes, 2006

Punset, Eduardo: *'Por qué somos como somos'*, Editorial Aguilar, Biblioteca Redes, 2008

Punset, Eduardo: *'El viaje al poder de la mente (los enigmas más fascinantes de nuestro cerebro y del mundo de las emociones)'*, Editorial Destino, Imago Mundi, 2010

Punset, Eduardo: *'Excusas para no pensar (cómo nos enfrentamos a las incertidumbres de nuestra vida)'*, Editorial Destino, Imago Mundi, 2011

Ratey, John J: *'El cerebro: manual de instrucciones'*, Editorial Arena Abierta, 2002 (first published in English as *A User's Guide to the Brain*, Little, Brown, 2001)

Rodríguez Delgado, José María: *'Mi cerebro y yo'*, Ediciones Temas de Hoy, 1994

Rodríguez de Rivera, Ignacio: *'La Mente del Mundo'*, Bubok Publishing S L, 2009

Rubia, Francisco J: *'El cerebro nos engaña'*, Ediciones Temas de Hoy, 2000

Rubia, Francisco J: *'El sexo del cerebro' (La diferencia fundamental entre hombres y mujeres)*, Editorial Temas de Hoy, 2007

Small, Gary y Vorgan, Gigi: *'El cerebro digital'*, Ediciones Urano, Barcelona, 2008 (first published in English as *iBrain: Surviving the technological alteration of the modern mind*, Collins Living, 2008)

Smith, Edward E y Kosslyn, Stephen M: *'Procesos cognitivos' (Modelos y bases neurales)*, Pearson Prentice Hall, 2008 (first published in English as *Cognitive Psychology: Mind and brain*, Pearson Education, Prentice Hall, 2007)

Tierno, Bernabé: *'Poderosa Mente (cuando cambias tu mente, cambias tu vida; la curación está en tu interior)'*, Editorial Temas de Hoy, Colección Vivir Mejor, 2009

Tirapu, Javier: *'¿Para qué sirve el cerebro?'*, Editorial Desclée de Brouwer, 2008

INDEX

ABOUT MILLWARD BROWN

At Millward Brown, we are passionate about brands. As a leading global research agency specializing in advertising, marketing communications, media and brand equity research, we have been in the business of brands for more than 35 years.

We have helped our clients build strong brands and services through research-based consultancy and today, we continue to push the boundaries of marketing research and brand consulting.

Our focus on all things 'brand' is fuelled by our clients' expectations for success and our own appetite for challenge, insight, solutions and innovation.

Firefly

Firefly was created by Millward Brown, bringing together some of the world's finest qualitative boutiques. We collaborate seamlessly to provide clients with the brightest creative and strategic research possible. Our single-minded objective: to drive brand success.